Just Passin' Thru

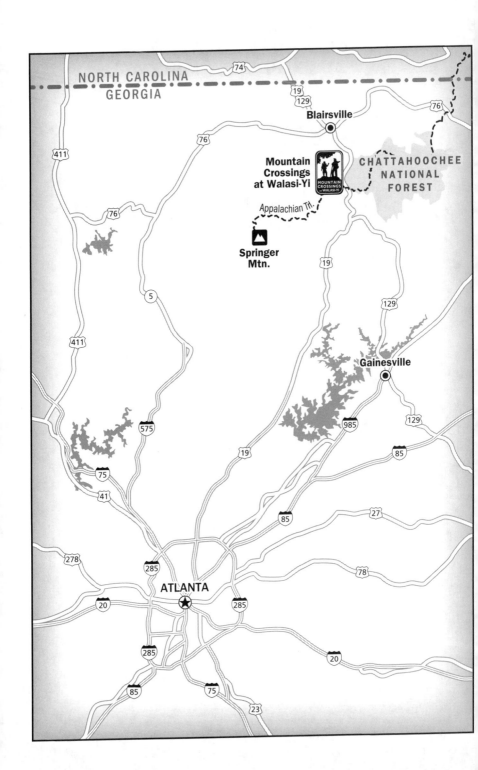

Just Passin' Thru

A VINTAGE STORE,
THE APPALACHIAN TRAIL,
AND A CAST OF
UNFORGETTABLE CHARACTERS

WINTON PORTER

MENASHA RIDGE PRESS
Birmingham, Alabama

Published by Menasha Ridge Press
Printed in the United States of America
Distributed by Publishers Group West
First edition, second printing 2010

Cover design by Scott McGrew
Cover and author photographs by Reed Wislar
Text design by Annie Long
Cartography by Scott McGrew
All other photographs courtesy of Mountain Crossings at Walasi-Yi
    and James "Alpine" Ingram

Library of Congress Cataloging-in-Publication Data
Porter, Winton.
    Just passin' thru: a vintage store, the Appalachian trail, and a
cast of unforgettable characters/Winton Porter.
        p. cm.
    ISBN-13: 978-0-89732-849-4
    ISBN-10: 0-89732-849-3
    1. Hiking—Appalachian Trail—Anecdotes. I. Title.
    GV199.42.A68P67 2009
    796.510974—dc22

                            2009036296

Menasha Ridge Press
PO Box 43673
Birmingham, Alabama 35243
www.menasharidge.com

contents

dedication

Marjorie, Sierra, and Allison Porter: *May you soar confidently in your own skies; dream freely in your own minds; make the impossible, possible; and remember to love yourselves first. The rest will follow.*

special thanks

William R. Porter, Directing Editor: *Carry your pen proudly. Your talent, brilliance, genius, and commitment to this project are nothing short of incredible. You are destined for great things. Let us all hope that you write about them.*

To the Porter and Julian families: *There is nothing greater than the encouragement of friends and family. Thanks for believing in this book.*

Billy Bumblefoot, Life Coach: *You have been the shadow that has lifted me up, dusted me off, and pushed me forward throughout much of my life. You have been that guiding voice that has taught me about compassion, humility, laughter, dreams, friendship, and love. Thank you, my wise friend.*

preface

In 2001 when my family and I came to live at Mountain Crossings—the little outfitter shop that sits astride the Appalachian Trail where it crosses Gainesville Highway outside Blairsville, Georgia—I brought with me a stack of cheap, coffee-stained composition books. These were the tokens not so much of a writer's ambition as of a hiker's habit. People who love the private experience of nature have to take special measures to preserve their memories of it. The swoop of a hawk, the slow lifting of mists from a valley at dawn, the release of the thickly sweet smell of pines after a storm: these things don't make the news. Unlike the fortunes of your baseball team or the sexual misadventures of your congressman, these aren't the kinds of experiences that Google and Wikipedia will remember for you. If you want a record of your journey in a wild place, you have to make it yourself.

By the time we made this move, I already had a long career in outdoor retail in Atlanta and Chicago and Salt Lake City, and I had been hiking the North Georgia mountains since I was a boy growing up here in the South. Indeed, like the visitors you will meet in this book, I myself had been a visitor to the old stone-and-chestnut store with the covered breezeway for many years before I became its proprietor. So I brought with me to the mountains a certain confidence that I knew what I was getting into.

No one was ever so fortunate to be so wrong. It has been eight years, and I have never once known what is coming next. Before long, my friends included one old man who liked to sleep on my roof and another who, well into his eighties, said he was still hiking just to keep from getting bored. An ex–Navy SEAL who lived in my basement and cooked breakfast for my guests was sometimes mistaken for a homeless person. My daughters, both of whom could melt their father's helpless heart at will by the time they learned to walk, were growing up gorgeous and smart in their new home away from urban life. Margie, my wife and my best friend, was becoming more beautiful to me by the day in the sanctuary of our new surroundings.

So preserving the stories of these people and these times in their lives and my life began to fill up my composition books, one after another, until I looked up one day and saw a stack that was a foot high. Together they would make a substantial thud if they fell off the desk. Thought, reflection, and memory have a very real weight, and what was I to do with this palpable substance?

I began to find the answer—and with it, the resolve to write this book— about a year ago, on a slow morning in early summer. I was watching the eyes of customers who milled around the store, and few of them were buying, but everyone was looking. I noticed that what their eyes kept finding, what captured their imaginations, was not the merchandise, not the new gear they could own and take out with them, but the weathered mementos that others had left behind. What held their attention were the postcards, the photographs, the letters, the magnificently beat-up boots on our "wall of fame." The store itself was a living book, a family album inscribed by generations of passing souls.

I now share these stories, because they were never mine. Like all life's blessings, they are borrowed. It is my hope that I've honored their many owners—the dreamers, the wanderers, my neighbors in the wilderness, my friends, my family, and the late, great Sky Dog—by passing them on.

Winton Porter
Mountain Crossings
August 2009

Author Winton Porter (middle left, in sandals) traded in the corporate world for life amid staff, family, and friends alongside the Appalachian Trail in the North Georgia mountains.

CHAPTER ONE
Dream Big . . . Real Big

Atlanta, Wednesday, September 22, 1993. I'm trying to concentrate on the teacher's assignment, but I'm distracted by the rain at the window. A slender stream finds its way through a cracked seal and feeds a puddle on the sill.

I am attending the first of three management courses that Recreational Equipment Inc. (REI) has scheduled for the week, as the final preparation before beginning my new job with the company in Salt Lake City. The task I have been given is simple: "In fifteen minutes, write down fifty things you want to achieve or do in your life." (The trainer running the session helpfully told me, "There are no right or wrong answers.") I stare at the blank sheet of paper, and the old silver Parker pen begins its usual propeller motion between my fingers, a habit that generally jump-starts my thoughts.

Nine minutes later, I've poured out a river of dreams and wants— plans, possibilities, fantasies. As it happens, I've also written down my own future on that page, as goal number twenty-two: "Own an outdoor shop in the mountains, with my Dad."

Fast-forward to May 15, 2001, at 1:33 p.m. At the very place, and in the very mountains, that provided the vision that moved my Parker pen, goal number twenty-two came true. I learned that if you can find your canvas, you can paint your picture.

This is the story of my crossroads canvas and the wackos, heroes, and friends who have passed across it like brushstrokes. It's their story, too.

The historic stone building where our story takes place is called Mountain Crossings at Walasi-Yi (pronounced "Wa-LA-see-YEE"), near the town of Blairsville, in the North Georgia mountains. It houses the outfitter, hiker hostel, grocery store, backwoods mail drop, gift shop, picnic spot, and sometime barbecue joint that is both my personal business and my former residence. Built by the Civilian Conservation Corps, beginning in 1934, the facility was finished in 1937, incidentally the same year in which the Appalachian Trail (A.T.) was completed.

The A.T. itself runs through the structure, down a breezeway separating the store from the residential building. This is the only place on the entire A.T. where the Trail passes under a roof. From here, it's about thirty miles to the A.T.'s southern terminus at the summit of Springer Mountain; it's about 2,178 miles to the northern terminus atop Mount Katahdin in Maine, thirteen states away. By my calculation, the climbs along the route between here and there, taken together, amount to twenty-seven Everests.

In the past five years, between 1,100 and 1,500 hikers have been venturing out each year to walk the entire Trail—according to the Appalachian Trail Conservancy (ATC). Most of them start out in Georgia in the cool of early spring and move north as summer comes on. Again according to the ATC, a majority of them (70 to 75 percent) will not make it all the way to Maine. But nearly all of those southern starters will reach Mountain Crossings, at the intersection of Neels Gap and Gainesville Highway, after a four-day hike from Springer Mountain. This procession of wandering souls over these years has provided me a window into the human spirit, in all its imperfection. What I have come to realize is that there truly are no ordinary moments in life.

While Atlanta, eighty-eight miles to the south, has undergone a rapid transformation from regional rail hub to sprawling metropolis, the old gray stone building hasn't changed much since 1937. A forest of 750,000 acres—of hemlocks, Fraser firs, live oaks, red spruces, mountain laurels, flame azaleas, and sassafrases—surrounds Mountain Crossings. Visitors from the city often tell me that they can smell the difference.

Mountain Crossings is situated at the base of Blood Mountain, the summit of which, at 4,458 feet, is the highest point on the A.T. in Georgia. There are various theories regarding the origin of the mountain's memorable name. Some believe, for example, that the appellation derives from the color of the lichens and Catawba rhododendrons growing near the rocky summit.

The more vivid and more locally popular account is that the name comes from a great Indian battle, fought on the mountain three centuries ago, in which the Cherokee defeated the Creeks and so claimed possession of a place they considered holy. According to this legend, the mountain was named for the blood of the fallen, and the battlefield was the place we now call Slaughter Gap.

Over the past three quarters of a century, the building has shared her covered breezeway with millions of people from around the world, starting with the three hundred young men of Civilian Conservation Corps Company No. 431 who built Walasi-Yi from 1934 to 1937. The team celebrated the completion with a ceremonial passing through the breezeway on May 18, 1937. A long procession of wandering souls has left its footprint under the protective covering since then, wearing a smooth groove in the old stone footpath that stretches exactly seven casual strides.

Some members of this procession have become legendary among folks around here. Earl Shaffer, Crazy #1, is considered to be the first to hike the entire A.T. in one season, in 1948. Gene Espy, Crazy #2, repeated Shaffer's performance in 1951. Emma "Grandma" Gatewood may have been the craziest of them all. With little more than a shower curtain for a tent, an old army blanket, and a pair of Keds basketball shoes, she in 1955 became the first woman to hike the Trail: a sixty-seven-year-old mother of eleven, who would do it two more times by the time she turned seventy-five. The incredible Bill Irwin, with some help from his dog, Orient, became the first blind person to thru-hike the A.T., in 1990.

To walk on the Trail is partly to join the company of these legends, to share their experience. But people have their private purposes, too, the things they can't share. I meet men and women who take to the Trail because they are courageous, or half crazy, or lonesome. Often they are determined to prove something to themselves, and very often they are just too stubborn or foolish to imagine they might fail; sometimes they just drift into the woods because they don't mind where they go. I believe that the Trail offers an experience of life on the level that was intended for us: life away from the misery of traffic jams, the cramp of cubicles, the senseless arrogance of tall buildings. I have plenty of customers who must disagree. I see them wandering in the parking lot with their cell phones, looking for the magic patches of service, asking each other: "Are you getting reception?"

But the breezeway does not discriminate. It welcomes us all—it puts up with all the different visions of itself. That makes Mountain Crossings no ordinary place.

One of my first unusual experiences happened one early morning in late May of 2001—just after I took over the shop—as I was preparing for an early run up Blood Mountain. The sun was starting to crest the hills, and clouds were sitting very low, just above the roof. The effect of this combination was that the light of sunrise was refracted at a shallow angle through very low clouds, and golden light poured into the breezeway. (I've been fortunate to see this spectacular display on many mornings. I call it "God-light," since I can't help but imagine a high note sung by a heavenly choir when I see it.)

I was standing on the Trail in front of the breezeway admiring the light. I closed my eyes, took a deep breath, and tried to relax and absorb the moment. My stomach had been turning for months from the stress of buying the business, selling our house, and leveraging our family's entire life savings for a dream. It was the sort of strain that sets in after a big, life-changing move—as though I were struggling to remember, now that I was here, just why I had come. (What if I was one of those people who just drifted into the woods? What was my purpose here?) My wife, Margie, had been hesitant but supportive. If she didn't believe in what I was doing, she wouldn't let it show, but I knew she was nervous. Our four-year-old daughter, Sierra, had been asked to leave the comforts of a picket-fenced house, friends, trampolines, and swimming pools to live in hills full of banjos, backpacks, and long-bearded hikers who looked homeless to the eyes of a city girl. As for Allison, our second daughter, well, she was just a few weeks old and hadn't voiced any opinions thus far.

With my eyes closed, I moved into my pre-run stretching routine, first relaxing the neck, moving down to the hips, slowly reaching down to grab the ankles, then repeating.

It was then that I heard a voice off my right shoulder.

I opened one eye, thinking, Oh, shit, I must look like a freak standing here, twisting around like an idiot.

I opened the other eye and didn't see anything. I turned a full circle, but no one was around. I closed my eyes again and raised my hands above my head, trying to look less stupid if caught in a stretch move. The voice spoke again. This time I made out a few words.

The voice said: "Look up. Smile and dance."

No longer afraid of seeming foolish, I turned and said, to the air, "What?"

The voice repeated: "Look up. Smile and dance." It was barely audible.

I jerked my head to the left to listen. Now I was sure that the voice had come from behind me. At the same time, I started hearing drums beating beyond my left shoulder somewhere deep in the hollow. Forgetting the voice, or rather trying to shake it out of my head, I trained my ears on the rhythmic beat of the

At Mountain Crossings, the staff proudly shows off this 1934 photograph as part of its local history: Civilian Conservation Corps teams built Blood Mountain Shelter and the Vogel Lodge, and they completed a massive reforestation of Chattahoochee National Forest areas laid bare from mining and lumber harvesting. The lodge, which later became the Mountain Crossings store and facilities, opened in 1937. That was the same year the CCC completed, in Maine, the last stretch of the 2,178-mile Appalachian Trail.

drums, and I started walking toward the sound. I wanted a better glimpse of whoever in hell was beating drums at this early hour. The beat shifted behind me again, just off my right shoulder. I snapped my head in that direction and moved quickly. Now the sound seemed to be coming from behind the building. I had arrived at the balcony overlook when the drumbeat split. The sounds skipped off in two different directions and faded into the silence of the valley below.

For a moment I stood absolutely still on the overlook. A chill mixed with intermittent moments of warmth danced through and around my body. For maybe ten or fifteen seconds, it felt as if a group of tiny children, small as sparks, were singing, laughing, and running around and through me. When this euphoria lifted, my head felt light but clear, and my focus gradually returned to the landscape before me. Then, as I gazed over the balcony into the rich forest below, a new feeling relaxed me so much that my knees shimmied briefly. Again it seemed impossible to focus my eyes on any one thing. Then silence filled the air. I sat on that balcony for another ten minutes, watching and listening and trying to decipher the words. The sun started to rise over the edge of the ridge, greeting the lightly clouded valley below. What happened that day seemed to be an introduction to what lay ahead. Was it a welcome or a warning?

The voice and the drums have never returned. As I write this now, eight years have passed. I would be the last to describe what happened as a religious experience. Spiritual, maybe. Heavenly spirits didn't float over my head, and an image of Mother Mary didn't appear in a half-eaten PowerBar lying on the ground. The episode reached beyond religious connotations. I wasn't just a spectator, presented with something to worship. Instead I felt connected, for an instant, with everything around me at once.

After years of reflection, it seems to me that the voices and drums I heard that early spring morning confirmed or clarified that the decision I had made was sound. I had risked everything to pursue and live my dream. I had quit my high-paying job. I had ransacked our savings for every dime to buy this business, to purchase this inventory. After writing "goal number twenty-two" in that long-ago management class, I had made the choice to become a participant in my life, not just a spectator. It was a time to look up, to smile and dance—my own dance.

Shown here in black and white, The Mountain Crossings At Walasi-Yi is a 25¼" x 20" watercolor painting by Jessie Kay Collins. In photographic detail, it depicts the breezeway at author Winton Porter's historic store, near the southern terminus of the Appalachian Trail. Note the old stonework, where a white blaze (to the left of the hiker), marks the trail's passage beneath the roof that connects the store to the residential quarters and hostel at Mountain Crossings.

CHAPTER TWO
Pansy-Ass and Other Funny Plants

It's an unusually warm morning for early March, and weary hikers are starting to stroll off the Trail, cross the road, and stride into the parking lot of my store-hostel-rest stop. I've just returned from the hospital with a snakebitten hiker who goes by the trail name Brain Storm.

When I first met Brain Storm, he was standing by the stone wall on the back side of the breezeway, catching a smoke before bedtime. Pale-skinned and mostly naked, he was a natural target for snakebite: a lot of unprotected skin shining in the dark. He was wearing boxer shorts and white socks. I asked him where he'd hiked in from. He gave a courteous sideways blow of smoke, which caught the wind and covered me anyway, and said, "Gooch Gap, about fourteen miles back."

Just as I looked down to admire his white cotton socks, the copperhead that had admired them first struck at lightning speed from a crack in the masonry and sank its fangs deep and hard into Brain Storm's big toe. Just as quickly and silently as it had appeared, the viper slipped back into the crack.

Brain Storm felt the hit and started a shaking dance backward, screaming, "What the hell was that?"

I said, "It looked like a copperhead, but it could've been a rat snake."

"No shit," he groaned, hopping on one leg. He shoved the cigarette back into his mouth and grabbed his foot and kept hopping. "What am I supposed to do?"

"I suggest that we get you to a hospital to see if that bastard pissed his load into your bloodstream. You'll be all right, but we've got to move."

My words didn't calm his nerves completely. He lowered his foot back to the ground, but he couldn't walk, and he wobbled onto his knees and dropped to the ground. There wasn't much of a doubt anymore about what was or wasn't in his bloodstream—the only question was how much of it. I grabbed him under the arm and lifted him back up, helped him shuffle over to the parking lot, and steadied him carefully against my car before letting go.

Brain Storm yammered and moaned. "Damn it, damn it. This sucks. Should we tie a tourniquet around the toe or what?"

"No," I said. "What we should do, what we're going to do, is get you in the back of that car, get that toe situated below your heart, and get you to the emergency room, quickly."

Strapping a tourniquet on a snakebite is a cardinal sin of first aid. You stand to lose a lot more from cutting off blood flow than from a copperhead bite. Sucking the venom from Brain Storm's toe would have made a funny YouTube video, but it would have done little good in preventing the spread of the toxin. There was one quick home remedy that would have worked pretty well, and that was just slashing his foot off with my knife. But I don't think Brain Storm would have gone for that.

He had a lot on his mind. "I don't have insurance, man," he said.

"And if we don't get you down this mountain now, you won't have two feet, either," I said back.

He managed a nervous smile at this as I helped him into his seat. Another hiker, who had come running when he heard Brain Storm cry out, rode along with us and helped check the vital signs. We phoned 911 to alert the hospital that we were coming, and then we rushed down the mountain. Brain Storm had a look of confused feistiness, and that was a good sign. It meant that he was fighting back worry and fear, which usually catapult victims into shock.

He screamed out, "My freakin' toe is turning purple, and it's twice the size of the other one!"

With that proclamation, Brain Storm was starting to shiver slightly, which could signal that panic was starting to tear him down, and could lead to shock. I hollered into the backseat, "You're doing great. We're almost there. Stay calm." I stepped heavy on the gas and managed to take a few minutes off the twenty-five-minute trip to the hospital.

When we arrived, Blairsville's emergency teams were waiting. Two paramedics loaded Brain Storm onto a gurney and disappeared with him through the double doors. I waited for a couple of hours and was told that they could not administer an antivenin because they could not confirm that it was a copperhead. They would need to keep him for the night, hooked up to a saline drip to help wash out the venom. I saw Brain Storm in the hallway and waved to him as he was rolled into his most expensive hostel on the Trail.

The next morning, after I bring Brain Storm back into Mountain Crossings' hostel side, I climb the stone staircase and am greeted by a couple who, it turns out, have driven down from Rainbow Springs Campground in Franklin, North Carolina, to introduce themselves and provide advice on how to handle hikers. Whether I want it or not.

The woman is thin, mid-fifties, and stares at me as if she expects me to know who she is, even though I've never seen her before.

"Hi, I'm Jensine Crossman," she finally says, and gives me a stern look. She declines to introduce me to the man she has in tow. I reach out, shake her hand, and then extend it to the shadow behind her. Not surprisingly, he turns out to be her husband; name's Buddy—same as one of my guys who works here at the store.

"Great to see you," I say. Thinking I'll get some more information with a question, I ask, "Are you out for a hike today?"

"Oh, no, not me," says Jensine, just as Buddy is beginning to get his mouth open. "We just came to meet you and tell you about our hostel and drop off this flyer." Buddy reaches around from behind his wife and delivers an advertisement for their place. The marketing item turns out to be a piece of yellow paper with information crudely written, possibly by a child. Maybe one of their grandkids?

"Well, thank you," I say, doing my best to figure out whether I'm looking at a picture of a pine tree or a crocodile. "Have you started to get some hikers?"

"A few, but we're ready for them. We put new mattresses on the beds this year."

Now I'm catching on. This is the couple and the place mentioned about halfway through Bill Bryson's immortal book about the A.T.

"Great. I suspect that *A Walk in the Woods* really helped your traffic?"

Jensine's face turns red and her eyes bulge. It's clear that I've struck a chord. I'm about to learn to avoid this subject with her in the future. Bryson's book doesn't exactly flatter her, or her cooking, or her bunkhouse. Years later she's still got a grievance against that author, and she's making sure everyone knows about it.

"That fucker!" she growls. Jensine has a raspy voice, probably from years of cigarette smoking, and I suspect that she usually sounds irritated. Her favorite word, I also quickly discover, is *fuck*, in all its forms. Noun, adjective, adverb—sometimes she just throws it in for flavor.

For those who don't know, Bryson's A.T. hike led him to Rainbow Springs, where, for two days, he was trapped by a huge storm that slammed the Carolina mountains with three feet of snow. Neither the waylaid guest nor his overworked hosts could have been in a very good mood. Jensine and Buddy Crossman grumpily buried themselves in hikers' smelly laundry and went short on sleep, Jensine medicated herself with Marlboro Lights, and Bill Bryson went on to write a few prissy things about the smoke. He also noted that Jensine's

This vintage photo, on display at the store, captures Mountain Crossings at Walasi-Yi not long after it had opened, in 1937, as the Vogel Lodge.

chili was "pretty terrible" and described his nights in her "awesomely unlovely" bunkhouse as "wretched."

In subsequent conversations with Jensine, I've tried to get her to embrace the idea that there's no such thing as bad publicity, at least not when it comes to a write-up in a best-selling book for a run-down campground outside Franklin, North Carolina. But Jensine has a certain talent for staying angry. And maybe she just doesn't want to hear it from me, since I can't commiserate with her. Bryson didn't write anything harsh about Mountain Crossings, and anyway the shop belonged back then to Jeff and Dorothy Hansen, my predecessors.

"If Bryson were to ever walk into my store," Jensine says, "I'd tie his ass to a board, rub honey over him, and set him down by the river next to the bee box. That would sweeten him up a little."

"That bad, huh?"

"Bad? Are you fucking kidding me? That pansy-ass wouldn't know which side of the mountain to walk off when I was done with him. You know, he pissed off a lot of people along this trail, and he better not show his face around here again. Did you hear what he said about my chili? And the bunkhouse—what does he expect, the Hilton? With a Continental breakfast?"

Her barrage goes on for about five minutes, until she has to stop and catch her breath. She stands there, teeth bared, chest heaving, her cheeks blotched red-hot with anger.

"Well, he certainly has sold a lot of books," I say.

"Yes, I know, because tourists stop by our little store all the time just to get a glimpse at the rednecks behind the counter," Jensine mutters. "I'm from fucking Jersey, and this ain't no freak show. I think this is my last year. Mind if I smoke?"

I can't say no. I can see that she needs it. In order to light up, she must close her mouth. I take the chance to say my good-byes.

"It was nice to meet you, finally. Jensine, Buddy, I will send some hikers your way. You still take drop boxes, right?"

"No, no way," says Jensine, releasing a huge cloud of smoke. "We sell food. You should stop taking drop boxes as well. Your sales on food would go way up."

Oh, really? I can't hide my doubts about this.

"Oh yes, of course. You have everything they need right here. Don't you hate it when a big drop box shows up in the mail, and you know that you sell everything that's stuffed inside the damn thing? Stop taking them. Trust me. A little gem of advice—one you won't regret."

It is a busy day. More than a hundred hikers are expected to come in from the Trail, and as much as I want to hear more of her innovative business strategy, I need an exit.

"Well, it was great to finally meet you. I really should get back to work."

"Of course, come up anytime. We'll give you a place to stay."

As long as I don't expect a Continental breakfast.

At age four here, the author's daughter Allison welcomes spring in the storefront garden.

CHAPTER THREE
It Ain't About the Miles . . .

Margie jumps out of the bedroom, shrieking in terror. Her big brown eyes convey disgust, her screech means mouse, and the waving of her slipper—well, I don't know what that means.

"What happened? Are you all right?" I sit up on the couch, blinking. The TV remote slides from my lap and falls to the carpet among bald dolls and mixed-up shoes.

"No! No!" Margie shrieks. "I was putting on my slipper and couldn't get my foot in, and I kept jamming my foot—I was jamming it and, and—when I picked up the slipper and shook it and—A DEAD MOUSE FELL OUT!"

I try to hide my smile, but I can't, and she catches me.

"You think it's FUNNY?" she screams.

Four-year-old Sierra scrambles behind Margie to get a peek at the mouse and cries, "Mom, you hurt Mickey Mouse bad, but he still moving!" Our golden retriever, Sky Dog, runs over and sits at Margie's feet, offering her head for patting, and waiting for confirmation that her mistress is all right. Jezebel, the hyper tabby, appears on the scene, pounces on the dead mouse, seizes it in her jaws, and runs out of the room. Sierra screams, even louder, "Mom! Jezebel took Mickey and I think she is going to fix him and make him better, so don't worry." Margie starts to laugh. That laugh, so dear to me these many years.

We live above the hiker hostel part of Mountain Crossings on the Appalachian Trail. Literally on it. The hand-built, three-hundred-pound

American chestnut door of our home opens into the covered breezeway: our own five yards of the A.T. Just as the main store used to be a dance hall, the house connected to it was once the old Walasi-Yi Inn, and golden numbers from the hotel days are still mounted on the doors. Margie and I made a master bedroom out of Room 3, on the cold north side of the house. The baby, Allison, and young Sierra sleep in Room 1 on the south side, and Room 2, again on the north wall, is a fabricated kitchen consisting of a plastic sink, a stove, and a refrigerator. The den had been the inn's common area. The walls, floors, and ceiling of this room were of the same dark chestnut, which makes the atmosphere shadowy yet serene. The den also holds the primary heating system: an old stone fireplace with a bronze plaque bearing a dedication to Mr. Fred Vogel Jr. and August H. Vogel, the men who donated the property to the Georgia Department of Natural Resources back in the late 1920s.

The winters are hard. Whatever the temperature is outside, it will be about ten degrees warmer on the inside. On many nights, we have to put liquids in the refrigerator to keep them from freezing. It has become a family game to try to fight back the cold: tacking sheets of plastic to the walls, nailing frayed climbing rope into baseboards, shoving cast-off sleeping bags into doorjambs. In the winter we just surrender the three bedrooms—close them off, and live huddled together in the den. We are afraid to light the fireplace until it can be inspected, and we don't have enough money to hire a chimney sweep. We run a small ceramic heater, and on a good night we can get the temperature in the room above fifty degrees, depending on the outside temperature. It is chilly, but it is our home.

Although there are plenty of days that provide reason to complain—of cold, or the mice in her slippers, or the spiders that crawl out of the drains—Margie rarely does. She loves the journey we are on, and she believes in me, even on days when I don't fully believe in myself. The joys, setbacks, celebrations, difficulties, and laughs of twenty-two years together—a relationship built from shared experiences and respect, a marriage and a passionate friendship—have formed the bond that will get us through these anxious times and keep us warm in the cold.

Margie has aged gracefully. She is astoundingly cute, stylish, and sexy, and now has added a hint of aged elegance. Her kindness and humor shine in her face. Her smile will melt anger. For more than two decades, she has been my best friend. I can't imagine my life without her.

As I search the house, picking up bloody pieces of the mouse—Jezebel didn't fix Mickey after all—a faint sound rattles against the door. It's the uncommitted knock that tells me that a weary hiker has wandered off the dark trail, doesn't know where else to turn, and doesn't know whether he should be here or not. I tack on a smile, unlatch the door, and greet the traveler.

"Hello, how can I help you?"

The man outside surprises me, after that timid knock, with a crisp, robust baritone voice. "Hi, I'm the Preacher Man, you can call me Preach, and I'm hiking to Maine, to spread the word of God. Could you tell me where the nearest Baptist church is around here?" His face is greatly animated as he speaks. He purses his lips; his eyebrows jump up and down. The movements suggest that he's been practicing them for years. So I'm thinking he's either a real backwoods Southern preacher or a guy who has worked pretty hard on his act.

I step into the breezeway, shutting the door so as not to let precious heat escape the house. "Nice to meet you, Preach. Here in the North Georgia mountains, if you want a Baptist church, all you need to do is pick a road. They all seem to lead to one."

Preach steps back, away from the massive door, giving me room. He wobbles briefly under his heavy, blue JanSport pack. Judging by the look of this pack—vintage 1972, external frame—he might have been a Boy Scout the first time he carried it. It's much too small for his big body now, and it's badly overloaded.

"Well, that's great," he says. "You got a phone book? Maybe I could call one, and they could come pick me up."

"Maybe, but it's Thursday night. Do you really think they would be sitting in the office at this hour, answering phones?"

"You got a point." He thinks for a moment. "What's your name, son?"

"They call me Winton."

"Is that your trail name?"

"No, sir. Some people call me Jez-bee, but you can call me Winton. It's easier."

That's good enough for Preach, who kindly spares me a longer conversation about how I got my trail name. I can see that he's too cold and footsore to show much curiosity. He holds up his fists, one by one, and blows into them.

I tell him that the hostel's closed, but I have a place where he can sleep. "Head down those stairs," I say. "I'll get a key."

My trail name is "Just Be," which, when pronounced with a Southern drawl, sounds like "Jez-bee." The name was given to me by a longtime friend, mentor, and teacher, who went by the name of Billy Bumblefoot. Hikers have been taking on trail names probably since traipsing across the land became a pastime. Perhaps it is a way to further separate ourselves from the world outside the woods, to break with our boxed-up lives, and to free ourselves to just be who we are. I rarely use my own trail name, and rarely share it on the Trail. But I always sign shelter and hospitality guest books along the Trail with the name Jez-bee.

Now Preach removes his pack from his back and tries to carry the cumbersome load to the stairs with one arm, hunching his shoulder up. I turn and go inside for the key to unlock the door below. When I come back out, Preach is standing at the top of the stairs studying his pack, which is now at the bottom of the stairs. "Divine intervention," he remarks with a chuckle. "The Lord snatched the pack from my hand and cast it down them stone stairs."

I escort Preach down the old steps and into the lower section of the building. The fifteen-bunk hostel below our little apartment has been closed for a number of years. Later I'll open it up again, but for now it serves as a storage facility for the store. Like bones decaying in a sad, lightless cave, old mannequins lie in pieces among the empty and disused bunk beds. I hold the door for Preach and gesture him into the main room. He pauses just inside the door and takes a deep breath, drawing in the flavor and musty smells of years past, then rubs his eyes with his hands, slowly and firmly, as if to reestablish himself in the present. "American chestnut, right?" he says, indicating the timber walls.

"Yes, sir. Built in 1937."

They used to call the chestnut the redwood of the east. Some surpassed one hundred feet in height and had girths big enough to drive a small car through. Work teams from the CCC, Franklin D. Roosevelt's Civilian Conservation Corps, harvested the big trees when blight threatened to kill them off. One of the beautiful things they built with the wood was my house.

Preach steps farther into the room. "Where is that couch?"

I walk over to the haggard brown paisley couch and sweep a few mannequin parts from the cushions. "This is it. Home sweet home, warm and worn."

Preach sits on the couch, pats the cushions on each side of him with his hands, and declares it perfect. "Better than that foam sleeping pad I've been on for the past four nights," he says.

I tell him I ought to get back to my family, and ask if there's anything else I can do for him.

"No, this is perfect, perfect," he says again. "You open at 8:30?"

"Yes," I say. "I will be there, and I can help you get that pack organized and fitted in the morning."

"Great," he says. "I made a few mistakes."

But he isn't talking about his pack now.

"I made a few mistakes. . . . I hear this is the place that will show me the light and the way."

Wondering where on earth he heard that, I have to smile. From the door I can barely make him out. "The light, maybe. But the way is all you, Preacher Man. It's all you. Have a good night." I turn and walk out, closing the door behind me.

With Preacher Man all tucked in, I climb the stairs to the breezeway. But the Baptist fellow's asking me about my trail name had set me to thinking about Billy.

Billy Bumblefoot has been a positive force in my world for a long time. He is an old man with a childlike spirit—unassuming, but confident, curious, and wise. Billy apparently has a house in Florida, but he is only an occasional visitor there. His real home is in the woods, where he spends most of his days. However, it's not uncommon for him to be seen roaming around Trail towns or sitting at a bar, sipping a bottle of grape soda, his favorite drink. He is a whimsical old man with a flowing white beard that waves just below his neckline. The little hair that he has always hides beneath an old, floppy Tilley hat, once black, now faded to charcoal gray, that has a rare Appalachian Trail logo patch that reads "Georgia to Maine" sewn into the front.

Billy is slightly built, but strong. I have never asked his age, although we have celebrated several of his birthdays. Margie always serves the same thing: one chocolate brownie with one candle, a shot of 'shine, a glass of milk mixed with Hershey's chocolate syrup. But my guess is that he is in his late sixties. He is probably as fit as any forty-year-old marathoner, and he can outhike most twenty-year-old kids. He carries an old, hand-carved hickory hiking stick, with his motto carved down the side in large, carefully scripted letters embossed with white stain: "Hi, I'm Billy Bumblefoot. Just passin' thru thank you."

Billy is quiet by temperament, and when he speaks he's deliberate and often funny. He has taught me a great deal over the years, but I think I've learned the most from his compassion for life and his humility. He always carries a tattered little notebook to record notes or thoughts. Once, in the shop, after

I had rattled off all the trips and accomplishments and miles I'd logged over the years, he looked at me—into me—pulled out his little book, and started writing. He briskly ripped off the sheet of paper and slid it across the table toward me. Then he smiled, winked, and got up and walked out of the shop.

His note read: "Miles, months, days, hours, and minutes are for those who choose to keep a scorecard in life. Son, someday you will come to know. . . . It ain't about the miles; it's all about the smiles."

Every day brings another round of "shakedowns" to load up and send back home for hikers, with Nate (left, front) and Winton (right, front) heading up the team.

CHAPTER FOUR
PowerBars and Olive Oil

Up on the breezeway, which is feeling colder by the minute, I spy another late-evening hiker, this one young, small, and thin. He's carrying an ultralight backpack and, facing away from me, doing a silly up-and-down dance to warm himself. As a play on the name of a popular model, the GoLite Breeze—imagine a nylon sandwich bag, with shoulder straps—my coworkers and I sometimes call such bags "GoFreeze" packs. The sad-looking thing probably holds about twelve pounds. It wasn't designed for much more.

I hail him. "Cold night, don't you think?"

The kid, startled, ceases his jerking dance and turns to follow my voice. "It's not that bad," he says, "but I sure could use some more food. I just hiked twenty miles today."

"Wow. That's a big day in these mountains. Where did you start?"

You could hear the shiver in his voice, but he's trying not to act cold. "Started at Amicalola yesterday and left from Hawk Mountain Shelter today." He has hiked more than forty miles in two days.

"Wow. Impressive. Got a trail name?"

"Yes. They call me Cricket. I made most of my gear myself. Ever heard of Ray Jardine?"

I've been expecting this question.

Ray Jardine is a controversial, and unquestionably great, adventurer, inventor, and author who, since he walked away from a career in aerospace engineering nearly forty years ago, has made a revolutionary impact in more than one field of outdoor recreation. First it was rock climbing. In the seventies, Jardine was the first man to free-climb the Phoenix route up the west face of Yosemite's El Capitan; he accomplished the climb with the help of a contraption he called the Friend, a spring-loaded camming device of his own invention. The Friend opened a new frontier in rock climbing, helping to conquer any number of ascents that expert climbers had considered impossible without pounding iron. How deeply does Jardine's influence run in today's climbing world? Well, spring-loaded camming devices are now produced under many names by many manufacturers, but climbers will still refer to them, more often than not, as "Friends"—the way you will call a facial tissue a Kleenex or a cotton swab a Q-tip. The first commercial models were sold to park rangers out of the back of Jardine's car.

By the eighties, Jardine had mostly given up rock climbing for other outdoor pursuits, but he kept his radical style and his engineer's approach. He developed a lifelong habit of pulling off incredible feats with homemade gear. It's amazing what you can do with a sewing machine and a background in rocket science!

Most outdoors people know something about Jardine, from having read—or at least heard of—his books. And if not, his Web site chronology documents a life of extreme adventure. By sea, he and his wife, Jenny (an exceptional outdoorswoman in her own right), have kayaked the Alaskan coastline and rowed across the Atlantic Ocean in watercraft that Jardine designed. On land, they have tandem-cycled across the United States and back, skied to the South Pole, survived more than four thousand skydives, sailed around the world for a few years, and hiked the "Triple Crown" of North American long-distance trails: the Pacific Crest Trail (PCT), the Continental Divide Trail, and of course the A.T.

For all those exploits and his contributions to rock climbing, it's as a backpacker and an author of guides to backpacking that Ray Jardine has had his broadest influence. After completing a hike of the PCT in the early nineties that took too long for his liking and left him a little sore, Jardine became convinced that the prevailing wisdom in backpacking was burdening hikers with unnecessary weight, and so he set out to lighten his load. His aim was to be able to spend more of his hiking day actually hiking, and less of it recuperating from the strain of lugging his stuff. Less gear, for Jardine, means less bodily suffering under the physical weight of the gear, and less spiritual suffering under the metaphorical weight of the gear, too: less tugging on various straps, less fretting about expensive shoes, and fewer material possessions to come between hiking and your experience of the natural environment. In the early nineties, over years of investigations and experiments and long hours at his sewing machine, Jardine refined a systematic approach to hiking engineered, to the last detail, to help hikers travel as lightly as possible. In 1999, he set out his "Ray-Way" principles in a popular book, *Beyond Backpacking*, that effectively launched the ultralight-backpacking movement.

Although Jardine has written and publicly said a good deal about his hiking philosophy and his hiking technique, at the practical level the Ray-Way is primarily a matter of hiking equipment. When the Jardines took to the A.T., they carried neither parkas nor sleeping bags, but rather hand-sewn quilts that were lighter than either and served the roles of both; they carried modified umbrellas, the springs and catches removed, so that they could hike in cool rains without sweating under rain gear; and because they didn't have much on their backs, they didn't need heavy ankle support, and so they hiked in running shoes instead of heavy boots. Ray's first piece of advice for hikers is not to buy expensive hiking equipment, but to make it themselves whenever possible. Now, instead of selling rock-climbing tools out of his car, Jardine sells sewing kits from his Web site: Ray-Way hats, packs, quilts, tarps, and more, for anyone who can sew them. His reputation is staked to the claim that you—the average hiker, whoever you are and whatever your level of experience—can make hiking equipment for yourself that will outperform the best commercially manufactured equipment at a fraction of the cost.

Since I make a good portion of my living and feed my daughters by selling commercially manufactured hiking equipment, naturally I take an interest in this point.

"Yes, I know Ray," I say to Cricket. So I've escaped the preacher and his sermon, only to meet a Ray-Bot. And he is blocking the door to my house.

"Yeah, it's great," Cricket says. "I'm only carrying twelve pounds, and I got all I need. Hey, you mind opening up the shop, so I can get some food?"

"Sure, no problem."

The Ray-Way places high importance on maintaining proper ventilation. Poor Cricket, covered in goose bumps, looks as if he's had all the ventilation he can take. So he follows me up the stairs toward the shop, never taking a breath, all the while giving me a sewing lesson—telling me all about the fabrics he used, the stitch patterns, and whatever else I need to know to be just like him. I open the door and step into the warm building, thankful to be inside. Cricket also looks relieved. Now he doesn't have to pretend he's warm.

I turn on the light, and Cricket continues his chatter as he scours the shelves for food. Two piles start to form on the counter. First, call it the "eat now" stack: Twinkies, MoonPies, Ho Hos, Ding Dongs, and, to wash it all down, Nestlé chocolate milk and a pint of Ben & Jerry's ice cream. The second pile is "eat later": PowerBars and a bottle of olive oil. I'm thinking, "Could it be possible that the Ray of Way was instructing his audience to oil up the PowerBars and shove them up you-know-where so you don't have to include it in your total pack weight?" Maybe I could interest the gentleman in a jar of vegetable shortening? Perhaps a nice box of bouillon cubes?

A picture is worth 2,178 words—the number of miles from start to finish on the A.T.

GoFreezers always seem to be in a hurry, and Cricket is in a big hurry. His mouth moves at a hundred miles an hour. His brain is doing about sixty-five. So he asks a lot of questions, and then answers them himself moments later. Then he bounces on to another subject. Talking with him, or listening to him, is like watching a game of Ping-Pong.

Cricket grabs a MoonPie, rips open the package, and tears into it like a starved child. Even with marshmallow streaming down his face, his teeth and mouth covered in chocolate, Cricket keeps talking. He even tries on some sarcasm, with his mouth full. Maybe the glucose rush has him feeling his oats. "Hey," he says, "I hear you go through people's packs around here and help them lighten their load. You want to go through mine?"

I don't know why GoFreezers love asking me this question so much, or what explains the gloating behind it. You might expect that they'd be a little more embarrassed to admit that they weren't the first to dream up the idea that less weight isn't such a bad thing. In fact, Mountain Crossings has been offering pack consultations since 1983, going back to the Hansens' time, when they owned the place before me. We inspect hundreds of our hikers' packs every year, tell them what they can afford to leave behind, try to keep them safe, and then we box up what they don't need and ship it home for them. My post office receipts tell me that we lighten hikers' loads by about nine thousand pounds per year.

I tell him that I go through packs for people who are willing to listen to good advice, and that my advice will probably be: one, to get a bigger pack; and two, to put more in it.

"You're crazy, man," says Cricket. "I got all I need."

"Fine with me," I reply. "The less you carry, the easier it'll be for us to haul your cold corpse out of the woods."

I'm not even sure he's listening, and I can't help but feel agitated.

What concerns me about the Ray-Way is that it recommends to hikers of all skill levels a style that only the very healthiest and most-experienced outdoorspeople have any business trying. The rest of the hikers out there—the ones who, when they come into Mountain Crossings, ought to be glad to run into an old-fashioned, retrograde hiker like me—aren't just buying stuff; they're investing in sound equipment. They're buying the considerable peace of mind that comes from not having to bet their own lives on their sewing skills. Before your equipment can spiritually oppress you, you have to know how it works.

While on my soapbox, I will say this, however: for Ray Jardine himself, the Ray-Way is an exhaustively researched and safely practiced set of weight-saving hiking techniques. But in the hands of others, the Ray-Way can turn out to be a foolish adventure in unnecessary risks, taken on by people who act like converts to a new religion. Practically speaking, very few GoFreezers actually have the skill to go ultralight (18 pounds or less), but they delight in showing off their gear or lack thereof. A GoFreezer will enter the store like a missionary landing on a desert island, looking for converts. He will not remove his pack until he has made a complete circuit of the store and established contact with all of his potential disciples. He will wait until some hiker or tourist stops him and asks The Question—"How much are you carrying?" That will be my cue to run, because then the GoFreezer will loudly give twenty minutes of show-and-tell, sprinkled with advice that is perfectly capable of killing a novice hiker.

A Ding Dong later, Cricket finally looks down at his watch and seems shocked and irritated that he has wasted so much time with someone who obviously just doesn't "get it." He crams the last Twinkie into his mouth, shoves the Ben & Jerry's into the top of his pack, and says, "Man, I got to put down some more miles."

It's 10 p.m., and I don't have the heart to tell him that the Trail will still be there tomorrow. He grabs his pack and tosses it over his shoulder, waves a good-bye, and heads out the door.

Three hours have now passed since the Preacher, and then Cricket, arrived out of the dark, and I'm more than ready to return to the minor warmth of our little apartment. Margie, Sierra, and Alli have fallen asleep on the mattress we have pulled into the den. I quickly and quietly close the door and pause inside to savor my good fortune, watching my family at peace.

The indoor thermometer tells me that the temperature is up—all the way to thirty-eight. I grab my sleeping bag and crawl onto the couch, replaying the evening in my head as I slowly fade out myself.

This backpacker surely needs one of the store's famous "shakedowns" to lighten his load.

CHAPTER FIVE
A Cold Snap

It was colder than normal this morning. A bitter north wind was pounding the house. The large plastic sheet that we had nailed to the wall, stirred by the drafts that were getting through, sounded as if it were breathing. The little heater had shut down, beaten by the cold, but the red thermometer display on it was still flashing. It registered the indoor temperature at only thirty-two degrees Fahrenheit. I rolled over and checked on the girls from my vantage point on the couch. Margie was lying on her side with the baby, Alli, wrapped tightly in her arms, and they both appeared comfortable under the large down comforter. Showing her golden retriever loyalty, Sky was curled up on the other side of Alli, helping Mom keep the baby warm.

Sky heard my movement and turned her head to me, as if to confirm that the baby was fine. But then, raising her head higher, she pointed her nose in the direction of four-year-old Sierra, as if to say, but you'd better check on that one. I looked toward where little Sierra was sleeping and immediately noticed her feet, lying where her head should be. Sierra had somehow managed to flip herself inside the bag, and her head was now jammed into the claustrophobic foot box. I was still taking in Sierra's predicament when she started to wriggle inside that bag; the contortions got faster, and were followed by muffled screams. Sky jumped up, whimpering at Sierra's kicking feet. Sierra's screams grew louder, stirring Margie out of her sleep. I stepped over the mass of people, grabbed Sierra's feet, and tried to snatch her out of the bag, but in her panic she was twisting and flailing, keeping herself stuck.

The dog saved the day. Sky took the foot of the sleeping bag in her teeth and started pulling, giving me the leverage to yank Sierra from the bag. Sierra popped into the cold room and went sprawling on the mattress; she immediately curled into a fetal position, crying. I reached down and scooped her up, wrapped her into the blanket, and held her in my arms, trying to calm her down. Margie was up on one elbow now, groggily trying to see what was going on. I laid Sierra carefully down on the mattress next to Margie, and Sierra began to calm down. Allison slept through the entire event. Sky made a last patrol to make sure everything was all right. She circled the room and returned to her place beside Allison. Mother, daughters, and dog were soon sleeping soundly again.

I couldn't drift off again, though. After I delivered Sierra from the sleeping bag, I discovered that I was up for good. I glanced at my Casio wristwatch: 5:58 a.m., elevation 3,102 feet, temperature 33 degrees Fahrenheit. Which meant that I was still on the mountain and that it was going to be a cold day. I'd had word from the rangers watching the registry at Amicalola that more than a hundred hikers had launched off Springer Mountain in the past few days, and yesterday's ridge runners estimated that at least sixty of them were within eight miles of the store. They would all push hard to reach Mountain Crossings today.

I step into the breezeway with Sky and quietly lock the door. A cool breeze slips through the corridor, and I zip my jacket up. I pull on some Gore-Tex mittens. Outside the breezeway, a carpet of fine snow covers the ground. I'm scooping up a fistful of the white stuff off the old stone wall, instinctively looking across the road to the Trail, when I notice a small beam of light from a headlamp leading a tall, thin hiker walking off the Trail on the south side of the road. It's a familiar stride, belonging to a white-bearded man who holds a single hiking staff that equals his height. His old Tilley hat is flapping in the wind.

I walk closer and yell out, "Bumblefoot, is that you?" Sky runs toward the shadow, tail wagging. Billy looks up as he reaches the parking lot, acknowledges my call, and kneels down to greet Sky.

As he comes closer, I holler, "Welcome back, old man. I heard you were out there, somewhere."

"Yep," he says, grinning. "Somewhere. I'll tell you, getting down Blood Mountain is a bitch in the snow." The toughest challenges in these conditions would have been close to the top, where the Trail passes over stretches of bare, slick rock. Also, many of the Trail's white blazes are painted on the rock over that stretch. So if the snow sticks up there, then a first-time hiker could easily lose not just his footing, but also the Trail itself. Billy Bumblefoot is no first-timer, though. He could walk this mountain blindfolded.

"Got some coffee for an old friend?" he asks.

I tell him that I've been planning on making some, just as soon as I shovel some salt over the stairs. I ask him to grab some wood from the pile, and tell him that I'll meet him at the front door of the shop. Then I salt the stairs and the walkways and head for the door, eager to get out of the bitter cold air.

I hold the door for Billy, and he goes into the shop with an armload of firewood and starts to build a fire in the stove. I come in behind him and head for the back to turn on the lights and grind and prepare the coffee, a Brazilian roast.

I check on Billy. "Need anything?"

"Might want to grab some more of that wood. This ain't going to last long."

"Got it. Coffee's brewing in the back. Help yourself."

I grab a load of wood and start back to the store. Hurried by the cold, I'm not paying enough attention, and I step on a patch of ice outside the breezeway. The wood flies out of my hands and over my head, and I land flat on my back in snow-filled flower beds. Sky runs up to investigate the situation and starts looking me over like a mother checking for bruises. She's sympathetic but stern. Her eyes seem to say: you idiot. Slowly, carefully, I stand up and gather the wood and return to the store, trying to forget the episode. I find Billy in front of the counter, sipping on a cup of coffee from the same Superman mug that he has carried for years. He looks up and strokes his long beard and says, "Took a spill, did ya?"

I'm stunned. How in the hell does he know? "You some kind of wizard, old man?"

"No," Billy says, chuckling. "It's just that you either took a fall or you knocked the shit out of your head on purpose. That's a pretty good-sized gash on your forehead, son."

I reach up and feel warm blood making a slow drip along my forehead. "Damn that bear. I thought he was carrying a knife. That son of a bitch."

Billy starts to laugh, pulls a paper towel from the dispenser, and hands it to me. I ask him where he's been, since I haven't seen him in almost a year.

"On the Trail mostly," he says. "Thought I had found a girlfriend, but she ran off with a model from New York. No big deal. I'm too busy to be tied down anyway. How about you—everything all right at the Crossings?"

"Everything abnormal as usual. What does the traffic look like behind you?" With Billy here, I could collect the best information available. Nobody passes him on the Trail.

He laughs after another sip of coffee and says, "You got some good ones headed your way. I say you should have at least two rescues before noon. Then again, there's one I'm thinking of who might not even let you rescue him. He's carrying at least sixty-five pounds and ain't got a lick of food with him. I'd say he's more or less set on getting himself killed."

"Did you give him some food?"

"Tried, but he said he was going to live only on so much as the land and the Good Lord would provide, like the other creatures of the forest."

Even in the dead of winter, the author makes the Blood Mountain shelter his morning-run destination.

"Well. If I were a bear, I'd tell him he's got a deal."

"He'll be all right. He had one of them Tom Brown survival books. If he gets real hungry, maybe he could eat it." Billy nurses his coffee, raising his eyebrows as he does so—remembering something. "Almost forgot. I gave him a trail name. Di-Puts. I told him it was the name of a great Cherokee hunter who was so fast that he could snare a leaping rabbit in full sprint with his own hands."

"You think he's figured it out yet?"

"That it spells stupid backwards? Not a chance."

The snow is still falling on the mountain when the sun, in the distance, starts to rise above the gap, spreading a brilliant light over the pure white snow in the valley, a golden shine that accentuates beautifully the dark shapes of the bare trees on the slopes in front the building. Billy sits next to the fireplace, sipping on coffee, now writing in his old, tattered leather journal. What is he writing? Except for that one page he tore out to give me long ago, I don't know, and I never have asked him. Maybe someday.

Around 8:15, the staff starts coming in. Buddy (not to be confused with Jensine's husband, Buddy Crossman), as usual, is first, and he stumbles through the door, quickly slamming it behind him as if to push the cold away, and immediately shouts into the hollow air of the store in his harsh, barking Jersey voice, "Those damn Floridians have no clue how to drive in this crap!"

Buddy retired to the North Georgia mountains from New Jersey, on his way to Florida. He decided that his passion for fly-fishing and mountain air suited his lifestyle better than shuffleboard, tennis, or golf. Short, bald, stout, older than I, and always in his photosensitive eyewear, Buddy can be gruff and caustic, and his Jersey accent only adds to the pungency of his attitude. But the greater part of it is bluff and bluster, sound and fury. At heart, he's a gentle guy who loves fishing, animals, and his wife, Linda. One night he rolled his car off the mountain, swerving to avoid hitting a bear on an ice-slick road. For some days after the accident, Buddy didn't know whether Linda would make it. That temporarily put a halt to his tough-guy routine. But Linda got better—and Buddy stayed better, but he still shows touches of his original Jersey sarcasm.

"Florida," I say. "Oh, crap, we got snow! You know what that means, Buddy."

"Yep. Every Floridian within three hundred miles is going to be heading our way, to make a snowball."

Billy looks up, shakes his head, and smiles. Buddy groans at his own joke and then starts to laugh, and I follow his lead. It's a Saturday, twenty-four degrees, the sun is coming out, sixty or more northbound hikers are headed our way, and hundreds of tourists are en route by car to play in the snow. The perfect storm, at the perfect crossroads, on a perfect day.

The popular shelter at Blood Mountain sits about 200 yards from the official 4,458-foot summit— the highest point on Georgia's portion of the Appalachian Trail.

CHAPTER SIX
Indian Artifacts

The two-mile tumble from the summit of Blood Mountain down to the store is one of the most grueling descents in Georgia and has laid claim to many blown knees and busted ankles over the years. To the unknowing—those who get to the top and think they've got it made—it's a nasty surprise. As far as your joints are concerned, the hike amounts to about four thousand downward hops, usually with nothing softer to land on than sharp, slippery, sometimes-loose rock. Today, nature has added a sheet of ice expertly camouflaged with a thin layer of snow.

Billy, whose eyes are still sharp, sees the panicked hiker first. The old man has taken his coffee to the front window and is gazing out at the snow along the Trail. Against the brilliant whiteness, coupled with the stillness of the bare forest, he sees the one thing that is both dark and in motion: the figure of a single hiker coming at a hurried pace, nearly a run, down the Trail from Blood Mountain without a pack on his back.

"Well," Billy begins, and then pauses to take a sip of coffee before finishing his thought, "it appears that you have your first emergency of the morning coming across that road."

I join him at the window and watch the stranger cross the highway and leap up the snow-covered stairs toward the shop. Billy and I back away from the door in unison, knowing that the man's entry will be dramatic and we'd best stand clear. And then something funny happens: the hiker, still in stride, throws his weight against the door and mashes his face against the window, neatly framing a picture of confusion and fear. He can't figure out the door's 1937-style latch, which requires the press of a thumb, not a twist of the wrist.

After a reassessment of the latch, he manages to get the door open. He crosses the threshold and stands before us, stuttering to get the cold words out of his breathless mouth. "There's this, this, this, guy. . . ."

That's how they all start, and that's usually where they stop, though the gender of the "guy" may vary. There's this guy, and he's in trouble. Just why the guy is in trouble—just who is responsible—the messenger never likes to say, or pretends not to know.

The fellow leans forward, hands to knees to catch his breath and regain some composure. Billy clears the silence with "What is your name, son?"

"Brittle."

Brittle's about six-foot-four and drastically thin. He's somewhere in his twenties, but because of his underfed look, I can't say where. He has enormous ears that don't seem to match his long face or dimpled chin.

Billy continues his line of questioning: "Well, Spittle, what seems to be the problem?"

"These two brothers were trying to carry down this—thing—a big rock—strange rock-thingy. One of the brothers' back froze up on him, and he can't move. They said they'd been there a couple of hours."

"Did they have packs, sleeping bags, or tents, Twiddle?"

"Yeah, they had sleeping bags, and I saw a pack, but I didn't see a tent."

I look over at Buddy, who's standing by the counter with phone in hand, and give him the nod. He calls 911.

"Brittle, relax," I say. "We've got you covered, but we need some information on the guy in trouble."

We put the description together.

Age? "Late thirties."

Height and weight? "About six feet. Big guy. He had kind of a gut."

Was he conscious? "Yeah, but he was cold. They both looked pretty bad off from the cold."

Where were they? "About halfway up, near those steep steps."

Anything else seem strange? "Yeah. He kept asking me if I saw his shoes back on the Trail. But his shoes were on his feet."

Buddy says he has 911 on the phone. He looks over, waiting for instructions. I call out, "Male. Late thirties. Heavy, maybe two-thirty. Middle-stage hypothermia. Location: on the stairs below Blood Mountain. Send the board; we're sending two up now."

Buddy repeats my words into the phone in his usual loud Jersey tone, as if he were shouting a drink order to a Newark bartender. He hears the operator's short reply, then simply hangs up and continues cleaning the counter with his wet rag. "The order's in, boss," he says to me. "Should be here in about twenty-five minutes."

But we know that once they reach the store, prep the stretcher, and head up the trail, it will take another seventy-five minutes for the rescue team to reach the two brothers. I turn to Billy. "Want to go for a little hike?"

"Why not? I've had my three cups of coffee and two Snickers this morning. I could use the exercise."

"Good. I'll get my sack and jacket from the house. Go ahead and grab a couple more Snickers in case we're out past lunch."

"Oh, yeah! Free Snickers all around! Have one of these, Fiddle. It'll do you good." Billy gives Brittle a reassuring wink as he tosses over one of the bars. He's trying to keep the kid from worrying too much, but Brittle doesn't know what to make of him.

To Billy Bumblefoot and other discerning gentlemen of the woods, a Snickers bar is more than candy. Packed with calories, easy to carry, and delicious, it deserves to be called a perfect meal, or even a medicine, for the hiker's body and soul. Billy likes to say that a Snickers bar, in terms of health-giving powers, is like a steak dinner crossed with a Zoloft—except a lot cheaper.

"Better take a couple for our boys," Billy says, pocketing four more. "I'll do my best not to eat these before I get them up the mountain, Winton, but I'm not making any promises. See you at the stairs!"

Billy shoves past a bewildered Brittle and out the door, going up Blood Mountain with candy wrappers rustling in his pocket. I head next door for my emergency pack.

Of course, there's a story behind my pack. I'd been living on the Trail for all of three nights when I was awakened for the first time by a frantic late-night knock at the door. (It was a teenage girl wearing her just-crashed-the-car face. "We, like, took my grandmother up Blood Mountain, and it got dark on our way down, and, well, she's kind of like, legally blind, and we need more people to help get her down, and, like, we don't have a flashlight and could use another person or two. Can you help us?") Since then I've been keeping a ready emergency bag.

My old CamelBak M.U.L.E. pack holds the essentials: compass, headlamp, extra batteries, parachute cord, lighter, matches, plumber candle, three Esbit fuel tablets, two-liter water bladder, three PowerBars, three Snickers, glucose shots, titanium coffee mug, two tea bags, four sugar packets, poncho, fleece hat, gloves, two hand warmers, emergency blanket, two pairs of socks, bandages and gauze, pencil, notepad, and finally, duct tape, for handling the unexpected. In the winter, I add a silnylon eight-by-ten-foot tarp with tent stakes, a small Western Mountaineering down blanket, and a twenty-ounce thermos to the mix. Any or all of these things might be put to use on this trip. Considering the weather and Brittle's description of the victim, there's a good chance that we'll be dealing with a hypothermia case.

Think of hypothermia this way: it's what happens when your body, having already lost several battles with the cold, starts losing the war. The extremities are like abandoned outposts: the body sacrifices them and retreats to conserve its heat for the vital organs. That's why you can keep shoveling your driveway long after your ears and fingers have gone numb.

Hypothermia is what you get when continued exposure, like a siege, starts breaking down your thermoregulatory last stand. It begins when the core body temperature drops below 98.6 degrees Fahrenheit. There are three stages of hypothermia. The first stage happens between 98 and 94 degrees and is typified by chilliness, numbness of the skin, shivering, and dysfunction in muscle coordination, especially in the hands. At the second stage, between 94 and 84, treatment can get a little trickier, especially when core body temperature drops below 93 degrees. The hands no longer function; the legs wobble under any weight. The second-stage hypothermia victim needs a rescue. He can't hobble to shelter or build a fire, and, anyway, he may no longer remember where shelter is or how to build a fire; even the brain begins to freeze, sinking the victim slowly into delirium. He might be unaware of the shoes on his own feet.

Stage-three hypothermia, which begins when the body temperature drops below 84 degrees, is the most severe. The victim has entered the dead zone. The heartbeat is faint, the muscles are heavy and stiff, and the eyes—pupils dilated to a horrible width—start to take on the kind of calm that belongs only to soulless objects, like windows to an empty house. This zombielike state is the most frightening for the rescuer and requires precise, calm, and deliberate action. I've seen stage three once in my life, and I don't want to see it again.

Having hoisted my emergency bag, changed into better shoes, and grabbed a pair of trekking poles, I enter the woods behind Billy, making use of the track that he and Brittle have broken through the snow to ascend faster than these conditions would otherwise allow. I cover the first half mile quickly. My body is warmed by the ascent. I stop to pull off a layer, readjust my pack, and check my

A few of the Mountain Crossings legends gather on the balcony.

watch. It's 8:33 a.m. I'll reach the victim in less than thirty minutes; the rescue team is still, at this point, maybe an hour away from reaching the brothers. I plug in my headphones, and with J. J. Cale and Eric Clapton pushing my pace, I break into a run. Soon I manage to get within a hundred yards of Billy. Catching sight of me from a switchback, he acknowledges my arrival and, with a smile, lengthens his stride. I wonder how a man of his age can keep such a pace. He moves like a ghost floating through the forest.

When I finally reach him, halfway up the stairs, he's with the two brothers whom Brittle was describing. Billy is speaking with the one who's sitting on a rock, hunched over, fidgeting with the flip top of a crunched packet of cigarettes. The other lies on the ground amid scattered butts. There's this guy, and he's in trouble. This guy's trouble, in the first place, is that he's inside a cheap, flimsy flannel sleeping bag. Great for RV camping or for getting to second base at the drive-in, but in these conditions, it makes a better body bag than a tool for providing warmth. I grab the down blanket from my pack and throw Billy the rest of the pack without a word.

Billy digs through it, pulls out the lighter and one Esbit fuel tablet, and immediately goes in search of dry kindling.

I introduce myself to the guy sitting on the rock and ask him his name. He's shivering, and his teeth are knocking together, and he's trying to hide it. He speaks slowly and as precisely as he can: "My name is Mark, and this is my brother Peter."

Mark pulls out a bent cigarette and searches for his lighter through the many pockets of his undersized black and yellow John Deere ski jacket. Patting himself down, stroking his torso, he looks like a third-base coach going through the signs. I can see by his cap, which he tugs and tilts, that his favorite diner is the Waffle House.

Time to see how the guy in trouble is doing. "Peter? Is that your name?"

Peter opens his eyes slightly as I spread the down blanket over him and says: "Have you seen my shoes?"

"Nope, but we'll find them. No worries." His shoes are on his feet.

Since he's responding to questions, I've decided—gratefully—to place the thermometer in his mouth. (The situation doesn't warrant "going rectal.") I locate a faint pulse on his right wrist, position my watch, and start counting.

Mark has managed to secure his lighter. With his thumbs stiff from cold, it takes him a few tries to get a spark. He starts puffing furiously on his cigarette to get it started in the cold air. Training tells me that smoking can exacerbate hypothermia—nicotine contracts the blood vessels and reduces blood flow to the extremities, which is the same thing that the cold does—but then, ordering a guy in a Waffle House cap to put out a cigarette in the middle of the woods can cause other problems. If Mark's well enough to light up, he's better off than Peter, anyway. I let him smoke.

"I got sixty-five," I call out. "Time: 9:08 a.m. Temperature: ninety-three degrees."

Billy breaks from arranging the kindling to take notepad and pencil from the sack. He repeats the numbers: pulse rate, time, temperature.

The time registers in my consciousness. The rescue team is still an hour away at best. The vitals aren't great, but I'm relieved that I don't have to ask Marlboro Mark to strip naked and climb into the sleeping bag with his brother to warm him up.

Peter groans weakly. I ask him where it hurts.

"My back is locked up, and the top part of my legs hurts."

"It hurts? Or it's numb?" Hiker wisdom: if it hurts, it's still working.

"Sore. They tingle a little."

"Has this happened before?"

"Couple of years ago."

I grab his right calf through the sleeping bag and squeeze with my hand against it tight.

"Can you feel that?"

"Yes."

"Which leg? Right or left?"

"Right?"

He's correct, but he's missing the point. This isn't a guessing game. I repeat the question. "Right or left?"

"Right," he says. "Jesus, man. That hurts."

Much better.

"Have you seen my shoes?"

"Yes, we have your shoes. We put them back on your feet and threw in some toe warmers."

While I check for frostbite, I make small talk with Peter to keep his lips moving.

Peter works in a battery plant in southern Alabama and among NASCAR drivers he prefers Bill Elliott over Dale Earnhardt—something that he and his brother strongly disagree on. He was recently divorced after fifteen years of marriage and has two daughters: Katie, fifteen, and Jennifer, thirteen. He says that his wife ran off with some guy from Texas that she met on the Internet. His dad had taken him and his brother up Blood Mountain when they were kids, and he says that this place holds special memories. Well, that won't change, I imagine.

Billy has got a fire roaring underneath a small rock overhang, and we very carefully move Peter closer to the flame and work to make him a little more comfortable until help arrives. Mark moves next to the fire, takes a final drag off his cigarette, and tosses the butt into the flame.

"Fire?" he says, grinning. "What the hell do we need fire for? Figure we was warm enough before. Thought it was a heat wave. I don't know about this redneck here"—he gives the immobile Peter a brotherly slap on the chest—"but I couldn't stop sweatin'!" Mark breaks down in a fit of coughing and glad laughter. He realizes he's going to make it. This must be what the guy's like when he isn't afraid of freezing to death: loose, goofy, a good brother. His personality has thawed out a little, along with his limbs.

Billy sees a chance to get the story out of him. "Mark, what is it about this strange rock you were carrying?"

The hunk of stone lies victorious in the middle of the Trail. It's roughly cone-shaped, and there's a square indentation in the center of the flat face, the base, of the cone. I think I know what it is. Billy looks as if he knows.

Mark points at it and explains, "Yes'day, we found that there rock below the shelter on top of Blood Mountain. We're pretty certain it's some kind of Indian artifact. It must've weighed about a hunnerd pounds. We're thinkin' it's worth some money to someone."

Billy kneels down, studying the artifact, and runs a hand gently over it as if he were petting a friendly old barn cat. He stands up, shaking his head.

"Winton, you remember that big metal signpost that held that marker that was once on top of Blood Mountain? About fifteen years ago?"

"Yeah. They put it down in the parking lot at the shop."

"Well, this"—Billy kicks it with the toe of his boot, chuckling when gray dust crumbles away—"this Indian artifact is the old concrete footer that anchored that post. These boys were nice enough to bring it halfway down Blood Mountain for you."

Lighting his next Marlboro, Mark chokes on the smoke. He speaks with the cigarette bouncing in his mouth. "No shit? You gotta be kiddin' me."

"No sir," Billy says. "Me and about twelve others helped relocate the marker back in '88. I remember rolling this concrete footer over the rock cliff and watching it blast through the rhododendron thicket below the shelter. I can't believe you found the damn thing."

Mark stares ahead a moment. Then he twists from side to side, addressing himself, not just to Billy and me, but to the whole forest, in a loud voice. "Did I say I was the one who thought the thing was worth money? I take it back. Wasn't me." He's still coughing, but the three of us are laughing. He points at his brother. "It was his idea, man."

Peter, who is now much warmer but exhausted, simply closes his eyes in search of another dream.

Presently we hear the Union County Rescue Team below the ridge, and I start gathering my supplies off the ground. Billy tosses a few more small limbs onto the fire and stokes the flame with his hiking staff. He reaches into his pack, pulls out two Snickers bars, and neatly lays them on a rock in clear sight for the rescue team. I walk over to the concrete "Indian artifact" and push it off the Trail and down the snow-covered slope, watching it crash down the steep embankment toward its new home.

Rick Dyer is the first one to arrive. The leader and the fittest man on his team, he comes pounding up the Trail on his thick legs. He's built more slenderly from the waist up; the mismatch gives him a half-man, half-ox look.

He has a gruff voice but doesn't use it much, and he's chewing on a toothpick, rolling it from one side of his mouth to the other.

Rick's lineage goes back hundreds of years in these mountains, and many of the pastures below are owned by a Dyer or a Collins. These families regard the land as their permanent property. It's their home, their workplace, and finally their grave. They believe in their blood that they belong here more than others, and they do, in a way. I know that Rick will never quite trust or understand the hiker community, just as we would never be able to share his ancient, rooted point of view. We hiker types are just passing through, as Billy says. We're playing in these woods. And we don't worry so much about what belongs to whom, and how much of it, or for how long. Some of us don't even like owning much more than we can carry.

I hail Rick and ask him how many he has coming.

"Eight," he says. He fixes me with a cold look and spits. Then he steps around me toward Peter, who is now more alert and has stopped asking for his shoes.

I volunteer the vital information to him: "I got sixty-five and ninety-three degrees at 9:08 and now have ninety-five and seventy. It's 10:01."

"Did you go rectal?" Rick asks with a glare.

"No, sir. I did that last week with the other guy. You can if you want. Here is my stick." I pass the thermometer to Rick over Peter's head. "Sorry, Peter. You're in professional hands now."

Peter gives me a frantic, betrayed look.

"Peter?" Rick barks, pulling on a latex glove. "That your name?"

Peter nods, then closes his eyes. I stand up and back away and let Rick do his work.

"Rick, anything else I can do?" I ask, already knowing the answer from other experience with him. I'm considered no more a part of the Dyer elite rescue team than I am a member of the Dyer family. When they want my opinion or my help, they ask for it; when they're ready to give me my blanket back, they will. The rest of the time, I'm a ghost to them. This suits me fine.

Rick tells me I'm "free to go." When I thank him, I can't tell if he's listening. I slip on my pack and pass without a word, as ghosts do, through the oncoming crowd of uniformed men, who are short on breath and big in heart as they climb their final ascent to prepare their patient for transport.

Billy has already disappeared into the thick forest and is easily a quarter mile ahead of me. I'll let him go; he likes a quiet walk, and so do I. I take up a leisurely stride, enjoying the scenery that escaped me on the way up the mountain. I'm away now from the fire, from Mark's cigarette smoke, and from the scene of sickness and the scent of medical instruments. The clean sting of winter air in my lungs refreshes me.

Half a mile or so from the shop, I stop at a place we call Balancing Rock to enjoy some water and a Snickers bar, and a black bear cub stumbles out of the woods in my direction. My guest, still in the frizz and scruff of his first coat, is just a few months old; clumsy as a puppy, he looks friendly and confused. This is his first lesson about the smell of chocolate and peanuts. I bark to get his attention and move higher onto the rock in an attempt to locate Mama, who is sure to be close behind. I hear the sow before I see her, and I know by the sound of leaves and brush crashing under her weight that she's big and in a hurry. I stand tall on the rock and raise my stick above my head, trying to gain as much height as possible. She bolts into the clearing, snorting commands to her child. Again I bark, and now the great beast rears up on her hind legs as if to defy me in speech. The little one copies his mother's actions.

It almost seems appropriate to me, in this powerful moment, to say a word to these upright beings—"thank you," maybe, or "bless you"—but my training again does its job: I withstand the beauty of the bears, and my own delicious awe, in silence. We stand and look at each other for an interval I can't measure. All the usual timekeeping rhythms—my breath, my heartbeat—seem impossibly suspended. Then the little bear drops back to the ground and totters over to Mama, and the tension between her and me drops. Her panic and anger cool to motherly grumping. She scolds her cub with a few brisk huffs and noses him back into the woods. Behind him, she follows a few steps, then stops, reconsidering, and turns back to me. She gets the last word: a farewell snort and a wag of her nose, beneath which she may actually be smiling a subtle, benevolent smile, as if to say, *You are one lucky son of a bitch.*

Plenty of lucky men in these mountains today.

Sierra Porter, the author's older daughter, cools off by Helton Creek Falls, a pleasant hike from the shop.

CHAPTER SEVEN

Crawfish and Jambalaya

When I meet Chief, he's full of questions.

I'm following up on a mysterious signal from Buddy that Nate might need some help. When I heard this, I was just returning from an errand in town, and as soon as I entered the shop I could feel a tense hush in the atmosphere. That's an odd thing for Mountain Crossings air. Too many heads turned toward the door when I came in, as though everyone was waiting for me, and I heard voices in the back room. Buddy was at the register, and he pointed with his thumb, speaking much more quietly than usual. "Nate might need some backup," he said. He raised his eyebrows meaningfully.

Now, the customer-service end of what we do at Mountain Crossings often consists of smiling at people who have gone out of their minds. Nate happens to be very good at this job, because he is blessed with an even temper. His patience with customers is instinctive, genuine, and—almost—inexhaustible. When Nate needs "backup," it's a big deal.

In the back room, I find Nate helping one hiker with footwear, while another, a huge guy whose wet, musty gear is strewn all over the floor as though it were set out for a garage sale, hounds him with questions. I'm done dumping out my pack—will you come and look at it? How long do you think this is going to take? I don't see myself leaving any of this behind—shouldn't take long, should it? For the past five days, across forty miles of rugged mountains, this guy has lugged more than seventy pounds. The scales will give the exact figure, but I can see at a glance that it's more than he needs and that Nate keeps tucking and retucking a loose strand of his long, curly hair behind his ear. It's a habit with him that grows pronounced and jerky when he's mad. I can see my help is needed.

"Let me introduce you to Chief," Nate says. "He's from New Orleans."

Nate leaves us after making sure I've caught his ironic look: he's all yours.

Nate came with the place. We inherited each other—a legacy that enriched both of us. His sharp mind, athleticism, and can-do attitude made me like him instantly. In those days, he worked at the store four days a week and lived on the Trail the other three; he preferred a tent and a breeze over a mattress and air-conditioning. He also served as a ridge runner, hired by the Appalachian Trail Conservancy (ATC) to be, for the Georgia section of the A.T., a sort of peripatetic concierge, overseer, and educator in LNT, the Leave No Trace ethic. The job actually paid you to walk, and Nate loved to walk. He soon became one of my most trusted friends. He and his wife, Tina, were surrogate uncle and aunt to my two girls. Sierra and Allison would seize every opportunity to spend time with the couple, roaming through woods, dancing among the trees, looking for wild berries, or following animal tracks.

Nate and I worked together for six years, until he and Tina moved back home to Pennsylvania. They left my family feeling, for a while, too small and too quiet, while they found new challenges and new opportunities. We were happy for them; but from time to time it still feels to us as though two of our own are missing.

Chief is an enormous man who carries most of his weight in the middle. He moves with great consideration for his gut, at a backward-leaning waddle that thrusts it proudly forward; he is one of those courtly, portly Southern men who consider their girth a sign of dignity and wisdom. I expect a downright crushing handshake, and I get one.

"Nice to meet you, Chief," I say, returning the mightiest grasp I've got.

"Pleasure to meet you, Winton—Winston?—Winton," Chief says, bearing down hard.

We take the opportunity of this clench to size each other up. I've already noticed that he's favoring his back and also his feet. The latter must be blistered, because the soles of his black leather boots are being held together with duct tape. What I see better now is the jackrabbit look in his eyes. He's tired, he's out of his element, and he can't quite hide it. My impression is of a man who's used to projecting the image of a tough guy in charge; the Trail has given that image a beating. He's done his best to put himself back together, but the swagger has gone tenderfooted, the sweat isn't drying on his forehead, and his thinning hair, which back home would be a tidy comb-over, is all over the place. He's looking for someone he can trust, and my polite attempt to break his hand seems to encourage him. When he releases his grip, I feel I've passed some kind of test.

Gesturing at his mounds of scattered gear, I tell him we should be able to get him straightened out in a few hours.

"A few owuh?" he bellows in a Cajun baritone.

I nod, smiling. "First, I want you to break everything down into the following categories that are on this piece of paper," and I sound out my list to him:

Clothing	Personal
Water	Miscellaneous
Cooking	Sleep System
First Aid	Tent

Then I tell him, "I have got a small situation that I need to attend to, and I will return shortly. Do you have any questions?"

"Nope. I think I can handle it."

Chief was a hard-to-please hiker—and that's a more precise description than it seems. The hard-to-please hikers are a distinctive type of customer. They come in beaten, humbled, tired, and disoriented from carrying too much stuff, and then take offense when you suggest leaving any of that stuff behind. They're starting to wonder whether hiking will ever be fun. Some come in thinking they have the answers, others having forgotten the question, and many wonder, Why in hell am I still doing this?

The problem isn't meanness or stupidity, but self-doubt: the hard-to-please hikers don't believe they can be helped, by me or anyone. They don't know whether they're strong enough to keep going. Their first reaction to my store, my staff, and our services is a kind of self-pitying scoff—Do you honestly think you can help me?—that gives our ability too much credit and, at the same time, not enough. Too much, because we were once inexperienced hikers ourselves, and we don't know anything that's beyond them to learn; not enough, because what we do know can help them, despite their doubts. My work with these people takes the form of self-defense, then. I have to persuade them that what I am doing is not absurd, that my staff and I are not fooling ourselves, that we really can help them travel faster, more comfortably, and more safely along the Trail—and that they really are strong enough to keep going.

Attending to my "small situation," I drink a cup of coffee at the overlook, enjoying a moment of calm before I return to Chief. I find him seated on the floor, going once more over the checklist, scratching his head.

"Chief, thank you for your patience. It gets a little crazy around here sometimes, and things don't always go as planned."

"No problem," he says. "I got nothing but time."

"So you're from New Orleans? What did you do there?"

"Police officer with the NOPD. Ninth Ward. For thirty years." He pulls

The author (right) catches up on news with hiker and frequent Mountain Crossings visitor Paul Renaud, known by his "Ole Man" trail name. Paul and his wife, Jaime ("NaviGator"), own the Appalachian Trail Lodge, in Millinocket, Maine (www .appalachiantraillodge.com).

out his badge and proudly shows me an ounce of nickel and two ounces of leather.

I take the badge and inspect it. "How long have you been planning this trip?"

"Years! I finally got the time to do it."

"How do you feel about your decisions?" I glance down at the now neatly stacked gear.

"I feel a little stupid. I really think that I have too much stuff, but I can't think of anything that I can get rid of right now."

I tell Chief that his badge won't impress a bear much, but his gun might. We'll start with that.

Often the hikers who benefit most from Mountain Crossings' "shakedowns"— our item-by-item, ounce-by-ounce pack consultations—are those who start off feeling embarrassed by the process, as though it were a variety of indecent exposure. Spreading all you've got on the floor, waiting for a stranger to tell you what your possessions reveal about you, can be intimidating. Unfortunately, many hikers, by the time they reach our shop, have come to expect doubtful looks and scolding from others. Their friends have told them, "I can't imagine living five and a half months in the woods." Their colleagues have asked them, "What about your job?" Various others have called their actions lunacy or irresponsibility—often the same souls who raised them and fed them. What these hikers need is a welcome, and so we try to make the shakedown a welcome to serious hiking. We do what serious hikers do: we talk about what they're carrying and why. Which gear they need and which gear they don't need, yes—but also which lucky charm, which book, which favorite sweater.

A GoFreezer might have hard-and-fast rules about what can and can't be carried, but we don't. We try to balance the well-being of the hiker's back and feet with the needs of the hiker's soul. A Baptist hiker will never mail his Bible home, and a cop will hike with his gun. Billy Bumblefoot hangs onto the hardwood staff he loves, even when, as he knows perfectly well, it alone outweighs a pair of the latest carbon-fiber trekking poles. Once I pointed out as much to him, and he said, "Then I guess the stick will hurt more when I smack you upside the head with it."

It's not just a lighter pack that eases the load, after all. It's knowing there are people who don't think walking in the woods is crazy.

"Where's your gun, Chief?"

He shifts his weight from haunch to haunch and drops into a low, hesitant voice—"Uh, my gun?"—like a child who has just been caught with a firecracker in his pocket.

"Yes. What is it? A Glock 22, or a 22C?"

"It's a 22C!" Now his voice relaxes. The gun talk gives his features a happy glow.

"Smart choice. It's a little lighter by about half an ounce and has less recoil. Did you bring the ten- or fifteen-round magazine?

"Only ten," he says—adding, like a good student, "it was lighter."

"Nice. We'll just have to work around it. The entire thing will weigh about twenty-nine ounces with a loaded magazine."

Finally satisfied that I'm not about to try convincing a thirty-year police veteran to send his gun home, Chief relaxes his shoulders and leans back on his hands. We spend the next two hours assessing the need for every piece of clothing; every bandage, cotton swab, and pill; every match, lucky charm, and lashing strap. I try to talk him out of gear that he thinks is necessary, such as the thirty-six-inch machete or the bricklike *FM 21-76 Department of the Army Field Manual: Survival*. He gives in after a while, once he's changed the subject and spun another tale of his days on the force. He has me understand that New Orleans, like the saloon in *Star Wars,* is the scene of more or less constant murder and mayhem. (He seems to take a little pride in this.) He needs the gun, he says, because he put a lot of bad guys in jail, and now they're out, dozens of them, and they want him dead. He tells me exactly how John F. Kennedy was assassinated. (The kill shot, he says, was from the storm drain on the north side of Elm Street.) He's been married to the same woman for thirty-five years: Brandy. He swears many times that Brandy is the best cook in the history of the world. Back in New Orleans, Brandy is waiting for Chief to recover from what she considers a spell of temporary insanity and come home. She believes that if the Good Lord had intended us to go from Georgia to Maine on foot, He wouldn't have given us cars.

After repacking and checking the fit of the pack, Chief and I walk over to the scale. I flick on the switch to light up the digital pad.

"Okay, Chief. Moment of truth. Take off the pack. What do you think it weighs?"

"I don't know. A lot less. Maybe forty-three pounds."

"I would say that we are at about thirty-four pounds, with the gun, ten rounds, food, and no water."

I set the pack on the scale. The figures swing crazily for a moment, and then it reads: 33.5. "Good thing this isn't *The Price Is Right*," I say.

Chief steps back from the scale, eyes wide, shouting happy Cajun noise. I can tell he is impressed, but I have no idea what he is saying. Something like: "Lookadat! Fa-troo?"

"What?"

"Fa-troo? Fa-troo?"

For true?

"Yeah," I say. "I don't think that scale's lying to you."

Seizing my hand again, he now gurgles his thanks, pumping my arm as though he wishes, in his gratitude, to rip it right off. "Y'all are jus' amazin'! Gawd, ah didn't think dat'd happen! I los' twunny-se'n pounds!"

When I get loose of that horrible grip of his and assure him I've been glad to help, he smacks me heartily in the shoulder and demands to know what he can do for me in return. "Maybe sump'n from N'Awlins!" he suggests. "What'd you like?"

"You don't have to do that," I say.

"Naw"—he wallops me again—"but I want to! Whadjalike?"

I think for second. "Well, I ain't ever had crawfish. Send me some crawfish sometime."

This delights him, and he promises he'll send some "dressed, straight from da Quawtah." I assume he means the French Quarter. I don't know what "dressed" means. I never do find out exactly.

The other shakedown that day is thirty-six-year-old Mickey Cascarilla of Los Angeles. (We learn exactly how old he is because he asks us to guess. I say thirty-two and make his day.) We tag him with the trail name Casper. He is originally from New York and followed a girlfriend out West. She got a role in a sitcom on ABC; he, too, planned to make it in "the industry." The relationship fell apart about three months after their arrival. He did a few toothpaste commercials and had a few one-liners in some no-name movies. It didn't pay the bills, so he decided to sell real estate. He did that until he burned out.

"—and now I'm here," he declares, correctly enough. "Where am I again? Am I still in Georgia?"

Casper bought all of his gear, with the exception of a cigarette lighter, from a Big 5 Sporting Goods on Wilshire Boulevard. It's a mess of bad choices. First he selected, for his body's six-foot-two frame, a kid's pack; then he picked out a discontinued-model stove from a closeout sale. He didn't pay much for this stove, but then he shouldn't have, since there probably isn't a replacement fuel canister for it anywhere in the United States. The arm on his crank-to-charge flashlight snapped off in the cold, and his cotton-poly sleeping bag is soaked right down to the paisley fleece lining. His water filter froze on its first night in action; the swelling ice put a three-inch crack in the casing. His tent—which, he was proud to say, he got on sale for $29.99—is sixty inches long, or fifty cents an inch. It wouldn't have been a bad deal if he'd been a foot and a half shorter. His clothing is mostly cotton, with two exceptions: his long underwear and a leather jacket that weighs about five pounds. It's my first tough-love shakedown of the week.

"Casper, this is crap. If you keep moving through these mountains with this stuff, we are going to be carrying your frozen corpse out in that wet sleeping bag. I hope you kept the receipt."

"Oh, yeah," he says. He reaches into one of his jacket's fifteen pockets—the operation involves a lot of Velcro and zippers—and produces a foot-long strip of paper.

"How did you spend $1,012.32 and walk out of that store with only two pieces of equipment worth keeping? And what's up with this jacket, man? This isn't *The Wild One*."

"Well, the guy who helped me said that he walked on the Trail before. He sounded like he knew what he was talking about. And I like this jacket. Come on. This is a nice jacket."

I shake my head. "I'll get a box for you to throw all this stuff into, and we'll send it back to Big 5 in the morning. The jacket goes home too, unless you plan on riding a motorcycle out of here. In the meantime, I'll pull some gear together and help you get safe again. *Capisce*?"

An hour later, having prepared about $800 in useless equipment for transit back to Wilshire Boulevard, Casper is smiling again. He thinks all his new gear is pretty cool; he'd never heard of Gore-Tex before.

He carries his things to the front counter to check out and meets Buddy. The late-afternoon hikers are starting to come in for a night at the hostel.

"Where you from, Buddy?" Casper asks.

"Jersey!" Buddy yaps, exaggerating the inflection for theatrics.

"Oh yeah? I grew up in East Orange."

Once they've traced each other's roots to the exact street corner, they exchange a series of personal insults. Apparently this is some kind of weird Yankee bonding ritual. Casper tells Buddy it's no wonder that he's bald and ugly, because he's probably the result of inbreeding, like the rest of his neighborhood. Buddy picks up Casper's new jacket and shows him which arm goes in which hole. A small crowd at the register is taking in the show.

Buddy rings Casper up on the register and calls out the total: "That'll be $653.38, East Orange! For that much even you ought to be able to stay alive a couple of days."

Casper flips through a stack of credit cards. "Here, try this one."

"What, you want me to blow on it for good luck?"

"If you think it will help."

Buddy scans the card, waits a minute, then cries out: "Declined!"

"Hey, Mr. Clean, why don't you say that a little louder?" Casper whispers.

So Buddy obligingly turns to the rest of the shop, now completely customer-packed, and announces loudly: "DEEE-CLINED!"

All eyes turned to the front counter.

"It's okay, everybody!" Casper yells. "I have another one!"

And with laughter and applause, Casper is welcomed.

Stalwart staffer Nate Helminiak heaves some ship-it-homers beneath Mountain Crossings' sturdy scale, used to weigh backpacks before and after the store's "shakedowns" for hikers.

CHAPTER EIGHT
Snow Day

Standing guard at the front walkway, her muzzle specked with frost, Sky Dog monitors a bustling winter scene. The parking lot is full, and children are spread across the front lawn building snowmen, carving angels with their bodies, packing snowballs. The snowball throwers are posted to each side of the stone stairs, and every adult is fair game. I'm no exception. Halfway up, I get pelted across the cheek from the right by a frigid blast from a five-year-old girl with blond hair. She wears a pink jacket and matching jester hat with gold bells dangling from the many points.

I turn, wipe my face, and, with a squinty grin, ask her, "Do I know you?"

She delivers a dimpled, gappy smile and informs me plainly: "No. It's a snow day, and you don't have to know me."

"Fair enough." I scoop snow from the ground, pack it quickly before she can escape, and return fire. Sky Dog joins in the folly before she quite knows whose side she's on, bunny-hopping through the deep drifts. She chases me a few steps, then turns and goes after my jingling opponent.

My daughter, little Sierra, shoots out howling through the front door of the shop and takes sides with the jester, and together they mount a frontal assault. Outnumbered and outmaneuvered, I try to counter, but my cause is hopeless. I take two in the chest, cry out desperately, and fall wounded. The two girls climb onto my back and triumphantly bury my head in the snow; I call for reinforcements. Sky Dog, sounding the bark of the cavalry charge, jumps on my back and sends the girls somersaulting into retreat.

After I rise to my feet (slowly and groaning, while the victorious girls laugh at me), I brush the snow from my nylon coat and promise them in my best pirate voice: "I'll get you next time, mateys! I will get you next time!"

Sierra jumps onto my leg and hugs it, hanging on like a monkey to a tree. "Daddy, please stay and play with me. Please!" She comes up with an excuse for me: "It's a snow day; you don't have to work."

That voice, that smile, those curly locks are hard to resist, but I must. I stump along for a few steps and then start peeling her off. She's as sticky as bubblegum. When I break her grip on my leg, I find her now swinging from my hands. Eventually I settle on tucking her under one arm and tickling her with the other.

"Dear," I say during this little wrestle, "I would love nothing more. But I must work today. Maybe next time."

Tickled out, she drops to the ground, stamps her foot, pouts—then sticks out her tongue and runs off with her new friend.

The shop is packed with customers and guests. I nudge through the crowd to the counter and tuck myself in behind it with Buddy, whose face is a useful instrument. It can register a whole range of colors from pink to purple, the precise shade depending on the number and mood of customers. Right now it's a good, rich crimson, which means a lively day for business, and he gives me a quick rundown.

"Nate's taking care of a shakedown in the back—with a guy who actually seems to know what he's doing. And the ambulance's here for some guy named Ricky, not Tony. And we got a report that some kid poured a bucket of snow in one of the toilets."

"Thanks, I think," I tell him, as I inch away from the counter.

"Oh, and one more thing," Buddy says. "Felicity's out on the porch trying to convince someone's wife that her husband and child are running late and not frozen dead on the Trail."

"Did you hear the woman's name? The one with Felicity?"

"Bridgette!"

Stepping out again onto the front walkway, I notice Billy in the garden, taking cover behind a silver trash can. He has picked a snowball fight with an army of little people in bright, puffy clothing. By the two five-gallon buckets full of ammo beside him, it's evident that Billy has planned his battle carefully. He's inflicting heavy casualties when Sierra springs from behind a fence post and gives him a beard full. He goes sprawling, and they all scream like fools.

It's ten-fifty in the morning, and the temperature has risen to about thirty-four degrees. Soon they will be running out of snow. I think: Growing up is truly a waste of precious time.

Felicity is one part wildflower, the other part bobcat. Slight in stature, with a petite nose speckled with fading freckles of summers past, Felicity is, as her name suggests, a woman who brings happiness to those around her by always being her own person. Looking at her, dressed as usual in a nonchalant array of fleece, nylon, and hiking boots, few would know that she used to be a Goth girl. And few would expect this diminutive young woman to be as tough as she is. But those who have crossed her—male or female—have witnessed her steely stare and stepped back from her fiery personality. She draws comfort from the care of her young son, six at the time of this writing, plus a keen interest in naturalistic and spiritual topics such as astrology and new-age philosophy. Her trail name is Cola Monkey, which is a product of her addiction to Coca-Cola.

The tall, slender woman beside Felicity is Bridgette, who appears to be in her late thirties. She has pale hair the color of maple wood, cropped straight across just below her ears. Her lips are trembling in the cold, and her eyes show the nervous weariness of a concerned mother. Bridgette drove up this morning to pick up her husband and son, who went out on an overnight hike. She waited in the parking lot for an hour, reading a book in the driver's seat, and then came into the store, upset.

"I need help! My family, where are they? They must be in trouble; they were supposed to be here over two hours ago! What should I do?" she yelled, and my staff calmed her down. She had stayed up most of the night worrying, she said; this was her son's first camping trip, and the last time her husband went camping was more than thirty years ago. She tried to describe the "neon-colored" pack her husband was wearing and noted that before they came up to the mountains they got brand new Walmart sleeping bags that were "really lightweight."

A lightweight sleeping bag probably made for an uncomfortable night, and it has been a very long time since good hiking equipment was regularly manufactured in "neon" colors. But there was no reason to panic. The staff gave her coffee and got her to wait another twenty minutes before she stormed into the store again. Now she's out on the patio, and Felicity is talking her down.

"When was the last time you spoke with them?" Felicity asks.

"This morning. About, I don't know, seven o'clock?"

"What did they say?"

"They said it was cold and that they were on the way out. Then the cell phone went dead, and I tried and tried to call them back!"

Felicity knows the Blood Mountain terrain better than most. She flips open her cell phone to check the time. It reads 10:53 a.m.

"You dropped them off at Woody Gap yesterday, right? What time?"

"Yes, about twelve, why?"

"If you dropped them off at noon yesterday at Woody Gap, they would have made it to at least Byrd Gap, which is about five miles in from where they started," Felicity says. "If they left Byrd Gap at seven o'clock this morning, considering the conditions, they should arrive here in the next thirty minutes to an hour." Felicity tosses in the extra half hour for cushion.

What is important is that we know that they are moving. That means they would be all right. Hikers who die in the middle of the Trail get passed—

and noticed—by other hikers. So do hikers who collapse from hypothermia. Since no one has rushed in this morning to tell us that a man and a boy are dying in their tracksuits in the woods—since, in fact, all of the latest customers have told us they've seen two people fitting the man and boy's description alive and still trudging along—we have every reason to expect that the woman's family will be fine.

There are better and worse ways of getting this point across, of course. I'm glad that Felicity has managed to do it without using the word hypothermia or collapse or dead. Trouble would have worked well enough. That's a phrase I use a lot in these situations: If they were in trouble, we would have heard by now.

I take a place at the chiminea. For the third time this morning, Bridgette refuses my offer of a bagel. Felicity and I have nothing to do but to wait with her and, as parents ourselves, to share her ache. We are confident that her husband and son will be out soon, but it is too much to hope that our confidence will rub off on Bridgette. It's not a pleasant thing to tell a mother just to wait for her son's safe return. The odds are very good, but it's not my child or Felicity's child we've entrusted to the odds. My child is playing with other kids a snowball's throw away; Bridgette's child is still in the woods, and she's not really interested in calculating his chances against frostbite, snakebite, bear attack, dirty water, rock slide, or lightning strike. Hiking is about managing these risks. Parenting—the fantasy of parenting—is about reducing risks to nothing.

Mercifully the wait soon ends, when four figures with backpacks come marching down the few final yards of the mountain before crossing the road. One is a young child, maybe nine or ten, only a few years older than little Sierra. I cross the front of the building and descend the long stairs to greet them.

The little boy crosses the road on the heels of his father like a mindful duckling. But once they reach the parking lot, he playfully pushes his father aside and gallops past him, as if trying to touch the imaginary finish line first. The boy reaches the stairs and pauses there when I call out to his father.

"You wouldn't happen to be the husband of a Ms. Bridgette?"

"Yes. Is she still here?" He's exhausted and ashamed. I remember Preacher Man's honest words. I made a few mistakes.

"She's on the porch. And I believe that she will be very, very happy to see you both. Follow me."

The boy speaks up brightly. "Mom's here, Dad? I hope she bought me some more Oreo cookies."

"That would be nice," the man says. Then: "Did you have a good time, Joey?"

The father's fear—and I have felt it too—is that his child will not forgive him. But Joey sees nothing to forgive.

"It was the best! I never saw so much snow!" He leaps up the stairs and runs ahead in search of his mom.

"Past the front door, Joey—she's on the deck!" I shout.

I stop at the door, and the man stops beside me. He is delaying his reunion with his wife, allowing his little soldier time to work some magic. To assist him in his thoughtful tactic, I introduce myself and offer my hand.

"Hi, my name's Winton. Where are you folks from?"

"Oh. Yes. Um, my name's Tony, and we're from, ah, Florida. Up for the weekend."

I figure that ought to hold me for a while. We let a few seconds tick by, while Joey disappears around the corner. We hear his piping voice telling Bridgette about "adventures."

"Would you like a cup of coffee, Tony?"

"Ah, yes. That would be nice, thank you."

"Sugar? Cream?"

"Splenda, if you got it."

"Perfect." I give him a pat on the shoulder. "Why don't you check in with your wife, and I'll bring a cup right out."

I stumble back inside through a jostling crowd of customers, many

One of the author's family cats, Toby, holds her own against the puppy, Patches.

of them lined up at the counter with new gloves and hats in their hands. Just behind me come two hikers trying to shove their way in with their packs still on. Buddy lets them have it.

"Eh! Eh! Eh! You two! What's-a-matter with you, boys? You're knockin' people left and right. Get those packs back outside, fellas, before you knock over one of these pretty ladies."

The two men make an immediate about-face and slink out. The crowd watches silently. The customers closest to the cash register seem to stand up a little straighter.

I break the silence in my best Southern drawl. "Hey, Buddy! Put a little more Georgia in that Jersey, would you?"

Buddy snickers and helps himself to the last word. "I said please, didn't I?"

Felicity sneaks up from behind and taps me on the shoulder as I pour coffee. "Do you want me to get that?"

"Yes, it's for the husband. Thanks. Splenda, he said. And why don't you grab a pack of Oreos and a Blood Mountain patch for Joey."

"No problem."

"Thank you for taking care of Bridgette. It was better you than me."

"No kidding!"

"Maybe we'll give Buddy the next one," I say, and hope Buddy hears me.

Soon after, I pour another cup of coffee for my friend Cimarron, who is coming in on his second thru-hike. He'd turned eighty-two years old on his last one. He is having some problems with his pack and needs some adjustments. We manage to get a few more pounds out of his bag while we're at it.

Cimarron still stands a pretty straight five-foot-nine, and his well-planted silver hair still sprouts in every direction, like Einstein's. Only his hearing has gotten old.

"WHAT ARE YOU DOING OUT HERE AGAIN?" I scream at him.

"Can't stand sitting around the house," he responds, as he pours a cup of coffee and sips thoughtfully. "Family thinks I'm crazy, I think. But when you reach my age, they call it eccentric. It's like a free pass for crazy for the rest of your life."

He speaks slowly and in broken rhythms, taking pauses for breath in midspeech. The effect of this is to make him sound somewhat puzzled, but in a good-natured way: the world is getting to be too much for him, but he doesn't blame anybody for it.

"HOW IS THE BODY HOLDING OUT?"

"Good. I feel it a little more, but I'm not as young as I was last year." He takes another sip from his silver cup and winks.

"WELL, YOU CERTAINLY ARE AN INSPIRATION FOR ALL OF US. HOW FAR ARE YOU HEADED TOMORROW?"

"As far as my feet will take me. If by chance you see me lying on the Trail, just push me over the edge, so I'm not blocking anybody's path."

I tell him I'll spread the word, and we laugh. Some day-trip tourists, shopping for T-shirts and refrigerator magnets, seemed unnerved by Cimarron's sense of humor. He toasts them with his coffee cup.

Joey follows his parents as they wander a few turns through the gift shop. He stops when he finds an illustrated Trail guide, then sits on the floor, eating cookies, looking at pictures of other adventures.

Apparently, any worries his parents may have had about today's expedition are far from his mind.

In spring 2009, at age eighty-six and on his third Appalachian Trail thru-hike—2,178 miles from Georgia's Springer Mountain to Maine's Mount Katahdin—the robust fellow at left, trail name "Cimarron," paused for his regular visit with the author (right).

CHAPTER NINE
The Special Gift

A Tuesday: a polar wind pushes its way through the old stone wall to slap me out of a shallow sleep. I pull the comforter over my head and find myself alone beneath it. Margie must have decided to trade privacy and companionship for comfort; she left the bed in the night for a warmer place away from the house's porous north wall. Unable to sleep but reluctant to move, I stay in the bed, drifting through random thoughts. I remember my run over Blood Mountain last week and thought I should run north on the Trail today. I wonder if little Allison escaped her crib again last night. Thoughts of yesterday's guests start crowding in—who they are, what they need, who will be safe and warm, and who will be victims of the bitter cold. I push them out, roll over, flip through mental pictures of mountaintops.

Now another stirring of air brushes across my face, but this one is warmer and going the other direction—toward the window, from inside the house—and this time it's not a breeze. It's from something that moves more precisely, carving a groove through the air: something flying through my bedroom. The hair on my arms bristles. I toss the blanket off and sit up in bed. A single bedside lamp reflected by the wood-paneled walls gives me a clear view of the room. I see a wide, winged shadow float across the ceiling and dissolve in the darker colors of the cracks in the chestnut walls.

My mind tries to interpret the aberration. Ceiling fan? There is none. An airborne handkerchief? A curtain floating listlessly from the rod over the window? There are no curtains.

Within seconds comes a deafening crash, and shards of glass fly through the air. My head jerks toward the window on the north wall, and I glimpse a red-headed bird falling outside the panes. It's a pileated woodpecker. And now the wind is whistling through a woodpecker-sized hole in the glass. I'm wondering if my day will be any better than his.

The door to the room opens wider. Margie enters, dressed in her usual sleepwear: a lilac down jacket and matching pants that fit her thin frame perfectly. They're from the fashionistas at The North Face. I doubt that Victoria's Secret could create an outfit more sensually splendid for a man of my taste.

I give her a flirtatious, bleary-eyed smile. "You look warm. Want to snuggle?"

She ignores the question and looks up at the hole in the window.

"Pileated woodpecker, right?" she says. "I thought I saw a flash of red go through the living room. Think he's dead?"

"I doubt it's dead. It's alive and well. Enjoying its idea of a perfect morning. I don't think I'm that lucky today."

She rolls her eyes, shakes her head with a grin.

"Come on. It's nice in here. I've got these warm blankets. Just a quick snuggle."

"You're not that lucky," she says. "You've got to get ready for work." She steps backward through the threshold and closes the door, gently.

Dryocopus pileatus, the "crested tree cleaver" of the North American forest, is the largest of the common woodpeckers. Its wingspan reaches twenty-six to thirty inches, and it stretches about a foot and a half long. It can hammer an incredible twenty strokes per second. Its thick, spongy skull and specialized cartilage, muscle, and membrane structures protect the bird's eyes and brain during this violent labor. For this tough-as-nails species (whose most famous member, the cartoon Woody, is a relative wimp), a windowpane is nothing more than an appetizer.

After installing cardboard in the broken-window space, I get dressed and walk over to the store. The woodpecker is gone, having left behind just a white-and-black tail feather on the windowsill. I half open the front door of the shop, and on cue Sky Dog squeezes through, swatting the door and then the door frame with her tail, preceding me into the dim interior. She checks the perimeter and returns to my side, tail wagging now against my leg. This is how she says that everything is safe. I rub the wall until I find the light switch and flick the lever. The aged lamps blink out a brief struggle against the cold air, and when the bulbs come on, they cast hardly more light than shadow through their steel grilles.

The smell of smoldering ash from yesterday's fire drifts through the air; I go to the source. The old iron stove stands proudly below the blackened stone fireplace. We call her Iron Maiden. She has dutifully warmed weathered souls for more than thirty years. I open her heavy doors, and they creak from age, like an old school locker. A handful of twigs, mixed with some dry leaves and a few small pieces of cured oak, kindle Iron Maiden back to life. I take a step back to admire the morning dance of flames jumping in the belly of the stove. A slight wisp of air curls the hair on my neck and beckons me to turn around. I hear the familiar rattle of the door's rickety latch. Damn—did I lock it?

The questioning face that comes peeping through the doorway belongs to Chief. He has freshened up his comb-over, still wet from the shower. He speaks in a whisper. "Are you busy? I wanted to ask you something very important!" He steps through the door and closes it carefully behind him. He moves slowly, quietly, deliberately—dramatically. I rub my eyes and yawn. It's too early for drama.

"What can I do for you, Chief?" I shuffle toward the coffeemaker.

He asks: "Would you bless me?"

This brings me up short. It takes me a moment to comprehend the word he's used. I'm not a professional blesser of things. This might be the first time I've heard this request in my life. "Bless you?"

"Yes. For Ash Wednesday?"

"But it's Tuesday, Chief. Mardi Gras. I think you got this whole equation backwards."

"Yes, but I'll be on the Trail tomorrow."

"Chief, I don't know nothin' about blessin' nobody, and I may be the last person you want blessing you. I'll drive you down to Blairsville today if you want. In the time it takes me to do some grocery shopping, you could get blessed fifteen different ways."

Intent on his sacred business, Chief can't be bothered to show irritation or amusement at my joke. He ignores it. He's not going anywhere.

"All you have to do is take this ash, put it on my head, and repeat after me," he says. This is no longer a request. These are instructions. He grabs my hand and smudges a nickel-sized blob of mud onto my fingers. It has the moist, grainy texture of dog shit. I sniff it distrustfully.

"I know, I know," Chief says. "Not ash. But I couldn't find any, so I scooped up some dirt from the garden. Just say what I say and place this on my head when I'm done."

Chief drops to one knee beside Iron Maiden and looks up into my eyes like a doleful retriever puppy. After positioning my hand inches from his forehead—making it hard for me to miss, I guess—he incants in his rich baritone: "Father in heaven, the light of your truth bestows sight to the darkness of sinful eyes! May this season of repentance bring us the blessing of your forgiveness and the gift of your light! Amen!"

I close my eyes, repeat the words as Chief says them. Arriving at "amen," I press my bit of dirt to his head. When the benediction is over, I open my eyes, only to see three people standing in the doorway looking on. They're neo-hippies, early-twenties men with half-grown beards. One's in a shirt from a Phish concert, and one has dreadlocks done up in a bandanna. The third one, who wears hemp bracelets on both wrists, looks a little less confused than the others. "Ash Wednesday, dude," he says, and the other two say, "Ohhhhhhhh, right on, yeah."

Chief rises from the floor and gives me a gentle hug of thanks. My eyes remain frozen on the three men in the doorway. I don't like the idea of being laughed at by guys who talk about "Jerry," using just his first name instead of the more respectful Jerry Garcia. Chief, blob of dirt firmly stuck to the middle of his head, tells them that I'm a "great man" and that I just blessed him.

"It's Ash Wednesday!" I scream helplessly.

"I thought it was Tuesday, dude," says Dreadlocks.

"Yeah, dude, but he's going to be on the Trail tomorrow," says Hemp Bracelets. "So he had to, like, deputize."

"Exactly," Chief says.

Nodding all around. Everyone's satisfied with the explanation. I'm still not sure the stuff on Chief's head doesn't have at least a little dog shit in it.

"Well, if it's already tomorrow, then I guess we're open," I say. "Come on in and make yourselves at home. I'll get the coffee."

Chief follows me to the back of the shop toward the coffeemaker. "Winton, you remember that I wanted to give you something. It means a lot to me, it's special, and I want you to have it. You have helped me more than you know."

This actually started yesterday. Every time I thought I'd gotten loose of him, he'd pop back into the store and make another profession of his gratitude. He followed me around most of the day, asking if I had a minute, because he wanted to give me "something special, in private." I hadn't had a minute, because it was the height of thru-hiker season, and anyway the request made me uneasy. The more he talked about giving me "something special, in private," the less I wanted to know what he had in mind. I had done my best to ignore him. I couldn't believe he was still after me about it.

"Come on, Chief," I say. "I helped you lighten your pack load, and I provided a little advice. No big deal. You'll just get a little farther along this strange footpath towards Maine."

"Exactly. That is why I want you to have this."

He extends his hand and slowly opens it, revealing, in a slightly muddy palm, a small picture of a woman, encased in a cheap, round plastic cover.

"Who is that? Your wife? Brandy?"

"No," Chief says. "It's Mother Mary." He lifts the trinket carefully with thumb and forefinger and holds it closer to my eyes.

"Of course," I say, once I've had a better look at the lady's costume.

"That's part of what I'm giving you. The other part's the story behind it." Chief tells the story.

"It was the winter of 1973, just after New Year's, 1973. Our precinct was dealing with a hostage situation in the downtown Howard Johnson on Loyola Avenue in New Orleans. Guy by the name Essex; ever heard of him?"

I hadn't heard the story of Mark Essex, or I had forgotten it a long time ago. Sometimes it seems that history doesn't disturb us in the mountains, that the big events leave us alone. But when history reaches us, it touches us with a special force. It costs something extra to carry stories to an isolated place. We meet the people who have paid that cost, who carry history to us. Many years ago, there was a young Black Panther named Mark Essex, who was full of anger and despair. Essex killed nine people in New Orleans, including the talented and admired Deputy Chief Louis Sirgo of the NOPD. Then the police killed Essex. They flushed him onto the roof of the hotel, and there, firing from the rooftops of surrounding buildings and from a helicopter, they put more than two hundred bullets in him. I learned this piece of history the mountain way: later than most, but from a witness.

"The man had already killed several people—grocer, doctor and his wife, three NOPD—and had fired on hundreds of officers with a high-powered .44 Magnum rifle, so negotiations were not an option. The fight was well into its eighth hour when my commander—well, he asked me and another deputy to follow him into the building. I was nervous, and I said so to my commander. He said, 'Don't worry. Cover my back, and we'll be fine.' This medallion saved my life that day." He holds it inches from my face and gives a sad, thankful smile, remembering. "See, every time I ever went into an uncomfortable situation, I'd tuck Mary into the underside of my watchband."

He demonstrates. Rotating his wrist, palm up, he tucks the piece carefully under the metal clasp of the black leather band.

"So, we're climbing the hotel stairwell, headed for the tenth floor. It was dark because power to the building had been shut off. He'd set fires in several of the rooms. We moved slowly. We were pausing at every landing. Once we arrived at the door, the door to the tenth floor, my commander took first position, and I took second, which was slightly behind and to his left. He flung the door open and extended his shotgun into the dark open space between the door and the hallway.

"Then there was this blast of light, appeared out of the blackness, this boom. Rifle shot ripped a hole the size of a grapefruit in my commander's abdomen. I raise my shotgun, all I can do is point it at that blast of light. And I swear the last thing I saw before returning fire was this picture of Mother Mary. The same one that I had under my watch. She flashed before my eyes, like she was there protecting me."

His eyes swell with tears as he points to the picture tucked under his watchband.

"I got off a few rounds, just shooting into the dark, and then I could hear the guy running away. Then I turned to my commander, who was lying on the floor, trying to hold on to what little life remained. Me and one other immediately grabbed his hands and feet and carried him back down something like a dozen flights out the door and into an ambulance. He was gone before we hit the back door. And not a day goes by that I don't think about him, pray for him."

Chief ends his story here. He looks up toward the ceiling and back down at his watch and then draws the little charm from his wristband and hands it over to me, saying, "That was a long time ago. I want you to have this. You have helped me more than you know, and this will help you, son."

So it's a funny transaction, on both sides. I accept a thing I don't know what to do with. Chief gives up a thing which he believes has given him divine protection for more than thirty years. I have to conclude that the gift—whether it really is a holy talisman or just a cheap trinket from some convent's jewelry sale—isn't the point. I get a close look at Chief when he presses his picture into my hand. He is giving happily. He is lighter by thirty-five pounds and one life story; he has unburdened himself.

Chief wipes his eyes in an attempt to prevent tears, but a couple get loose and roll down his cheek. He tells me he is leaving, and then he starts working on another one of his grand statements of thanks. This time, knowing what is coming, I cut him off the only way I know how, by clapping a hug on him. We squeeze and whack each other a few times. Then we go together through the front door and outside to the front walkway. Chief grabs his pack, now a much lighter version, with one hand, hefts it onto his shoulders, and starts toward the Trail. I watch him go.

Was this a man much given to a lot of hugging and weeping back home? Somehow I doubt it. My guess is that Chief's sentimental side is a surprise even to himself. That's what coming face-to-face with the thought of six months in the woods will do to you: as soon as you realize you have the chance to be a different person, you become one. You can forget who you are. This is no accident when you've spent miles wondering, with every labored step, Who is this person who has decided to try this?—wondering who you are. You have nothing but time to answer the question, to give a new account of yourself. Your only witness might be a blanket of cool moss on a sunny day, or a panorama of endless mountains, or a young doe grazing by the Trail. You've yet to discover that the journey is the destination. So you lose yourself, then you find yourself again, farther along.

It's possible that Chief gave up the protection of Mary because he decided that he was no longer the man who had needed her protection. And maybe my gift to him, then, was a new idea of good luck. In a box headed back to New Orleans that morning were his machete, his field manual. These things, he'd once thought, had protected him, too. He didn't need them anymore, either.

Later that day, when I fall into a trance at the overlook, watching mists burn off the slopes of the valley, it's the honking horn of the UPS truck that snaps me out of it. The truck has come to pick up Chief's box and many others.

The man in brown slams the brake and jams his truck into park. I see through the window of the large door that he is out of his seat and scuttling into the back before the truck, box-shaped and full of boxes, has stopped rocking on its wheels. Then the door slides open, and he leaps out, carrying a package about the size of two cases of beer. He bounds up the stairs, skipping half the steps, and meets me at the top.

"How are you today?" I ask him.

"Better today. Look forward to tomorrow. Tryin' to forget my past." He sets the package down and hands me his digital signature board. By the time I hand it back to him, he's carrying an outgoing load of hiker boxes tucked under his chin. "In a hurry," he says with a tight jaw.

He turns, leaps down the stairs, jumps into the truck, and roars down the hill. I look down at the package and notice that it's actually a hard-shell foam cooler. Stamped on the side:

URGENT OVERNIGHT DELIVERY
BAYOU BOUNTY SEAFOOD
BOUTTE, LA

A handcrafted pine emblem of the Appalachian Trail hangs by the store's front entrance.

CHAPTER TEN
Lorac

The morning silence of the woods is interrupted by the sounds of Collective Soul's "The World I Know" blasting from a sun-worn Isuzu Rodeo that charges into the lot spraying gravel. The vehicle is loaded with three bikes dangling from the back and two surfboards strapped to the roof. The Rodeo swings into a parking space, and out from the driver side leaps a man, wearing nothing but a pair of green-and-yellow plaid board shorts, who raises his arms above his head and greets Mountain Crossings with a roar of happiness.

"Winton, I am back! Ooh-rah!"

Master Sergeant James Ingram—we call him Alpine—has the energy of fourteen boys, the strength of five men, and the heart and demeanor of a child. He's fiendishly handsome, in a surfer way, with his golden-blond hair (close-cut, except for the wild sideburns) and a small strip goatee under his mouth, though he always seems as oblivious to his good looks as to his good fortune.

As for good fortune, Alpine owns three acres in Hawaii, two condominiums in Miami, property in Norway. He speaks six languages and can shoot the head off a squirrel at five hundred yards, with the "right rifle." He's traveled around the world twice and served two tours in Kuwait, two in Afghanistan, and one in Sudan. He's made successful climbs on three of the highest peaks in the United States: McKinley, Whitney, and Elbert. He owns up to two very close brushes with death: one in Afghanistan, when his platoon's helicopter was shot down, and one during a failed attempt to climb Nepal's Annapurna, the tenth-highest mountain in the world.

Hired in 2004, he has been working at our little store on and off for the past two years, having fallen in love with the place while on his first thru-hike in 2000. This is the first word of any kind I've had from Alpine in nearly eight months.

"You are supposed to be here at oh-eight-thirty, Sergeant. It's oh-eight-thirty-two. What seems to be your problem?"

"Screw you! Sir!"

I leap from the stairs and greet him with a hefty handshake and a man-sized hug.

"Welcome back to civilian life, jackass. Great to see you upright. How was Sudan?"

"I am done with the Army. If there is a hell on earth, part of it is located in northeast Africa."

The unwritten civilian code regarding military personnel is to not ask too many questions. Let the soldiers tell the story—what they want and when they want. It was Buddy who told me that Alpine had called and that he had been in Sudan on a "military operation"—what sort of operation, Alpine didn't say—for the past six months. Apparently, he had been back in Miami for the past four weeks, had gotten bored, and wanted to come back up the mountains and work. He said he'd load the truck and be with us in two days. His timing was perfect because we needed him. What else did we need to know?

"Alpine, I have to get this store open. We are expecting a fair-sized crowd today. We got the hostel back open and had about six hikers down there last night. Would you please check on our guests down there and get the towels in the wash?"

"Roger that!"

The hostel was located in a large section of the basement below our home. The previous owners, the Hansens, were forced to close it about five years ago because of problems with the drainage in the septic system. Once the problem was fixed, it took about ten hikers and two days of work—hauling out old furniture and broken mannequins, sweeping up owl pellets and mouse droppings—to get the hostel up and running.

This is the renovated hostel's first thru-hiker season, and it's starting to reclaim its old glory. The most encouraging sign is that the ghosts the Hansens told us about have already come back home. The busiest one is a woman we call Granny. We recognize her presence by her strange sense of humor. She likes to move stuff in the middle of the night and will toss dirty pans to the floor. Another is an old man dressed in Civilian Conservation Corps attire who's been banging on the old stone with a pickax.

It's middle March, nearly two weeks since Chief passed through the breezeway. The warmer weather has put an extra skip in the hikers' strides. It's Mother Nature's elixir: sunshine, a mild breeze, blue skies, low-seventies temperatures. As soon as it gets this warm, hikers start falling over themselves to mail their winter gear home. Mother Nature giggles and grins at such false confidence, keeping a few more cold snaps up her sleeve.

By midmorning, hikers and gear are spread all over the deck—on the picnic tables, along the old stone wall. Some have rigged their clothing up on bungee cords or odd lengths of hammock rope strung between low branches. Their fabricated clotheslines sway in the breeze, waving a virtual rainbow of nylon garments like prayer flags on top of a greener, warmer, smaller Everest. The topics of conversation that I overhear are the same as last week's, last month's. . . .

"Do you think I need this?"

"Sassafras, kick my ass, mountain was a bitch."

"Do you like those hiking poles?"

"And this hawk flew right over my head, screaming. I freaked out. It sounded like a missile."

"Does this blister look infected?"

"I am just not eating as much as I thought."

But people are talking faster and louder, excited by the sunshine. Everybody has a Trail story for everybody else.

Buddy steps onto the balcony with his coffee and stands next to me, sharing the scene. He takes a sip from his mug. "What do you think?"

"I think it's a beautiful day and that some of these people are going to make some very bad decisions about what they send home today."

"Yeah. What should we do?"

"Try to keep them alive."

Buddy makes the announcement in his usual tone, demanding the crowd's attention.

"Eh, eh, eh! All you peoples—yeah, you too, Goldilocks Boy. Part of what we do here at Mountain Crossings is to make certain that you don't die out here in these woods. If you have a question about sending something home today, you can ask my friend here. He's real good at keeping people from killing themselves."

I try to wave and hide at the same time.

A woman approaches, tips up her nylon ball cap, exposing her short white hair, and in a humble, quiet voice she says, "Hi. My name is Carol, and I could use your help."

Carol is a fit, petite woman in her early sixties. Her choice of clothing tells me that she doesn't lack experience. From the very beginning, she's generous with her smile, which has a way of both concealing her age and revealing it: the smile tender and innocent, like a child's, and yet it wrinkles her skin and brings out her autumn eyes, deep green and blue with tiny flakes of amber, in which there is something sorrowful. She has a steady gaze and doesn't dodge eye contact. She's used to having a man's attention.

I ask Carol what I can do for her.

"First, you can tell me—why is that man sitting on the roof?"

I turn, look up, and see Billy passed out in a lounge chair, wearing nothing but a pair of boxer shorts and cradling his signature Superman coffee mug between his two hands upon his chest.

"Ah. Oh. Uh. That's Billy, Billy Bumblefoot. He's okay. He just likes the view from up there, and he isn't partial to big crowds."

"Um—what's that sticking up between his legs?"

"Oh . . . Oh! That would be a flute. A Coyote Oldman flute, to be exact. It's rare. I think it's tuned in the key of C. What going on with your pack?"

"Well, I need to get some more weight out of my pack, and my shoulders are hurting more than normal."

"Let's take a look at it."

Over the next hour, we work with Carol's gear. She's already fairly light, carrying less than thirty pounds, so we're just trying to lose ounces wherever possible: cutting extra toothbrushes, eliminating packaging, tearing pages from her guidebook. There's a gallon Ziploc bag full of pills and pill bottles. "Eeny, meeny, miny, moe," she says, getting me to laugh.

The source of her discomfort is the pack itself. It's simply too large for her. There's no way to cut it smaller. We get a near-perfect fit out of a Granite Gear Alpine Vapor backpack. She loves it, and the total weight with food and water comes to a respectable and safe twenty-five pounds.

But a little while later, she will walk out in her old pack, though only after I've made her a deal.

First, though, I leave Carol for the moment and return to the balcony to check on the crowd that has continued to grow outside, and to make sure Billy hasn't fallen off the roof and been harpooned by his flute. Outside there's a group of about twenty Boy Scouts doing something more hectic than the usual milling around. I can see by the to-ing and fro-ing of those brown shirts and those awful yellow neckerchiefs that they're in some kind of hurry to get their packs off. They're pulling off gear and throwing it down in the grass in one big pile, as though they're planning a bonfire for it. Two men dressed in signature brown attire are climbing the stairs at a trot and headed in my direction. I smell them well before they get all the way up.

"How can I help you, fellas?" I say. "Actually—whoa—I could probably take a wild guess."

"Ah," says Scoutmaster One, sniffing himself embarrassedly. "Ah, yes. Um, well. Um. I was actually bit by the skunk, though. Do you think I should go to the hospital?"

"Bit by the skunk?"

"Yes, on the leg." He holds the leg out as far as he considers polite, under the circumstances, and repeats his question. "Should I go to the hospital?"

I tell him that would probably be a good idea and ask him how it happened.

"Well, I was in my tent last night, and I felt something brushing against my right leg, and . . ."

When he reached down, his hand landed on a warm and hairy thing. He grabbed the thing and threw it toward the tent's door, but the screen was zipped shut except for a bottom corner, and the skunk sprang off the screen in trampoline fashion and landed back in his lap.

"That's when I got bit on the leg," he says. "Not a happy skunk."

The man reached down again, grabbed the skunk by the scruff of the neck, and shoved it through the unzipped corner of the screen. He then crawled out of the tent in panic and discovered the skunk lying motionless on the ground. He went in search of a bag in which to dispose of the skunk, but when he returned, the skunk was gone.

"See, the skunk wasn't dead," Scoutmaster Two explains.

"And he came back that night and sprayed six of our ten tents," says Scoutmaster One. "Do you have any tomato juice and some water we could use?"

"He didn't spray you in the tent?"

"No. It happened so fast that I don't think it had time. Got lucky on that one. Could we use that hose?"

"Of course," I say. "And we have a bottle of Pole Cat Perfume in the shop that should take care of most of your problem." It used to be sold by a company called Ruff Wear. They discontinued the product, but we still have a few bottles. "Check with Buddy at the front desk, and he can get it for you."

Pole Cat Perfume is a mixture of hydrogen peroxide, baking soda, and laundry detergent. The mixture creates an effervescent cocktail that neutralizes the oils that bind the skunk scent to its victim. I don't think I've ever sold so much of it at one time, or seen so many people applying it to each other and their stuff. The Scouts take a spot in the grass by the entrance to the lot and stand around rubbing it on each other like sunscreen—then they rub it on their hair, their clothes, their tents. The most common skunk victim is the curious dog from the city who goes out on a day hike with its master and tries to make friends with forest animals. Never have we seen a skunk take on an entire battalion of Boy Scouts.

The deal I made with Carol had to do with her new backpack. When I come inside from watching the Boy Scouts' laundry party, I find Carol stuffing gear back into the ill-fitting old pack that had been hurting her. She sees me round the corner, and her eyes look sad, and I instinctively know that I need to break some ice.

I say, "You want to give that old pack another try? Good idea?"

She hands over the new pack, sadly. "Well, I really want the pack, and I know that I should get it. But I really just can't decide right now. Maybe there's no point—"

She stops there.

"Let's do this," I say. "You walk the three days over to Hiawassee. If you get there and decide that you want this pack, give me call. I'll bring it to you. Fair enough?"

"You'll do that?"

"Yep. If that's what you want."

"Okay, that will give me the time I need."

She lets go and sits back down to carry on with her task. At that same moment, Sierra bolts into the room, screaming "Daddy! Daddy!"

"This one must be yours," Carol says.

"Yes, this is little Sierra. She's seven."

"And a half!" Sierra reminds me.

"And a half," I correct. "That half is important to her."

"Nice to meet you, Sierra."

Sierra accepts Carol's handshake but is distracted by the small orange shovel lying next to Carol's pack. "I have one of those," she says. "We use it for digging poop holes when we go camping, but mostly I dig for worms in the front yard with it."

"Well, that's funny! I use it to dig up worms in my garden at home."

"Daddy? Daddy? I want to ask you something."

"What is it?"

Sierra holds out the palm of her tiny hand, exposing two quarters, and asks with great seriousness, "Daddy, if I give you fifty cents, would you play with me?"

I realize that people have purchased claims to my attention with much less than my beautiful daughter is offering. The moment before she asked this, I was looking around the store, scanning for customers, a businessman. Now I am a father on his knees.

"Of course," I say. "I'll play with you. Why don't you pick out some candy for us and go get your hiking boots on? I'll meet you back at the house."

"Yeah! Can we go up to Balancing Rock and climb and then maybe—if we like have enough time—go over to that old cave?"

"Sounds like a plan."

Sierra cheers, grabs some Snickers bars from the shelf, and runs out the door to get her boots on. I tell Buddy that I am taking the rest of the day off to play with my little girl.

Carol, who is loaded up now, walks with me to the breezeway. She drops some postcards in the mailbox, then shoulders her old pack.

I ask her if she has a trail name. She says she's never found one she likes. So I suggest Lorac. "It's Carol spelled backwards, and it's also like the name of the character, the Lorax, who 'spoke for the trees' in Dr. Seuss. I don't know why, but I think you are a voice for people who want to get out in the woods and play."

"I like that," she says. "Lorac works for me."

"Good. Give me a call if you need me."

Saying it to myself again later that day—Lorac—I wonder: to her, does it sound like the name of a drug? Eeny, meeny, miny, moe.

I meet Lorac at a motel in Hiawassee three nights later.

It's my second delivery that night. The first was of two sleeping bags to Tony and Greg, a father and son who had discovered that the lightweight sleeping bags their local outfitter had called thirty-five-degree bags and sold cheap were "not worth a damn after forty-five degrees." I had tried to explain earlier to the father: "You're going to get your ass kicked in the Smoky Mountains, if not sooner. Those sleeping bags are like bringing a knife to a gunfight." But the pair had walked through three sunny days and slept cozily through four mild nights before reaching my store, and they thought they'd be fine. After they moved through, Mother Nature drew those guns: three days and nights of freezing rain and high winds. Then Tony and Greg were ready for new bags. I had them meet me at the local grocery store, on the aisle with the peanut butter.

My next stop is the crumbling, mildewed Mull Motel, which—if you discount a rumor that the place got a new coat of paint in 1975—hasn't changed in more than sixty years. The caretaker who lives in Room 1 has been there as long as anyone can remember. Wherever exactly this hardworking woman is between age sixty and age six hundred, she gives you the idea, somehow, that she's been that age all her life. Without appearing to get older, she appears never to have been young, either; she just gets a little shorter and saltier every year. She's got a supernatural instinct for any threat to rules and regulations, and when I pull up to Mull's and let Sky Dog out through the passenger door, the caretaker pokes her head out of Room 1, clucking: "Hey! Hey, you! Mister! We don't allow dogs in our rooms here, and no partying after ten o'clock! Got it?" She doesn't wait for a reply and steps back into her room, slamming the door, like a ceramic bird popping back into a clock.

Lorac sits in a metal rocker on the concrete catwalk outside her second-floor room. She's reading her Trail guidebook by the lamp above her door, a little glass tomb of insects that casts a yellow light. Sky takes the stairs ahead of me and bounds up to Lorac with tail in full wag, as if she's known this woman all her life. I follow, carrying Lorac's new backpack.

"Don't get up. Sit down," I call out. Sky takes the invitation to sit as though it were directed at her and flops down across Lorac's feet. "Well, that is good," Lorac says. "I can't very well get up anyway with a pretty retriever sitting on my toes. How are you tonight, Mr. Porter? And tell me about that walk in the woods with 'Fifty Cents.' What's her name—Sierra?"

"That's right. I had such a good time, I decided not to take her money."

Lorac laughs. "I'm glad to hear that. That's the way to be a dad: cherish your time. Don't forget to lay claim to the moments that you have with her. They will be gone before you know it."

"Yes, ma'am," I say. "Your spirits seems to be up a little."

She smiles. "Despite the cold and wet weather, I actually had a great time out there. The gear is working—with the exception of the pack—and with each step I am getting stronger and more convinced that I can do this thing."

I tell her I believe she can. "My friend Billy Bumblefoot has a rule that he says all the best hikers follow: never quit in town, never quit going uphill, never quit in the rain. If you are going to quit, it has to be on a sunny day, on top of a ridge, with the wind in your face. You never walk away weaker, he says. You walk away stronger."

"That sounds like a good rule."

"Well, you can take that one or leave it. Remember, it's coming from a guy who sleeps on the roof with a flute in his lap. Let's check the fit on this pack and make sure you understand the straps and adjustments."

We go into the room. Right away I see the medicines again, the bottles out of their bag now and lined up—eeny, meeny, miny, moe—on the counter by the sink at the other end of the room. Sky, concerned as always for my safety, lies down just inside the open door of Lorac's room with her head sticking over the threshold, keeping a lookout. I instruct Sky to "hide" so the old woman doesn't see her in the room. She stands up, turns, and jumps onto the bed. She circles and settles in the middle.

"Sorry about that," I say to Lorac. "Sky, come on—up! That ain't much of a hiding place."

"That's okay! Let her be," Lorac says. "I'm no good at hiding either."

We spend the next fifteen minutes repacking Lorac's pack, adjusting straps and hip belt. "Think of your pack as a stick shift, not an automatic," I tell her. "As you walk, you'll be making adjustments with those straps all the time, depending on the terrain and what joint hurts. Do you want me to get that other pack mailed back home for you?"

"No, you can have it," she says. "Give it to another hiker who could use it. I won't need it again."

I ask her the question I've been wanting to ask. "Lorac, you're a cancer survivor, right?"

"No," she says—and I'm unprepared for this; I was expecting my next word to be a lame "Congratulations!"—but she says, "no, I am terminal." And I can feel my heart move in my chest. As though suddenly snatched by gravity, it falls, like a rock into water.

"Ovarian cancer." Lorac says the hideous words very quietly, protecting me from the sound. "My family thinks this is crazy. They're worried. But I have dreamed about hiking this trail most of my life. Last year was my first attempt. Made it to Virginia, got sick, went to the doctor, and was diagnosed."

Here she pauses, waiting for me to catch up to the truth. I can't speak.

"The part about dying doesn't bother me," she says. "It's the missing part that hurts. There's so much to say good-bye to. That might be why I'm on this trail. I'm saying good-bye to the earth underneath me, a step at a time. I've got some time left, and I'm going to take in the views, feel the sun in my face, and savor every step as if it were my last."

She reaches over, grabs the new pack, and starts stuffing her remaining gear inside, and I can see in her eyes and face the renewed commitment she feels. "I haven't told anyone about this since I stepped onto the Trail at Springer," she says. "Thank you for taking the time to help me."

Thinking I must have helped her mostly by being quiet, I decide to be quiet some more. I stand there a moment, suspecting that a hug is the next move but not sure. Lorac rises and gives me a generous, motherly hug. She lets go and sits back, rubs tears from her eyes, and says with a smile: "Now, don't you worry about me. You take care of your family and remember to lay claim to the moments you spend with those girls. I'll catch you on the other side someday."

Finally I find the power to speak, and to smile. "I have another play date back at the house tonight, actually. I think it's finger-painting night or maybe digging-for-worms night. I can't remember. I'd better get home. Best of luck to you. You're an inspiration."

Sky jumps off the bed and spends a few moments at the petting hand of Lorac as I head for the car. I open the door for Sky and call her. Lorac comes to the guardrail to wave good-bye.

"I want a picture from Katahdin for the wall, you hear?"

She says, "You got it! You got it." Laughing.

As I drive back home, I rewind the events of my hike with Sierra from three days before. She wanted to go to Indian Cave on the north side of the hollow. We bushwhacked down a steep hill and crawled through two rhododendron thickets. I had to carry her on my shoulder through a hundred-yard patch of briars before we reached our secret spot: It's a cave by the place where two creeks join and become one.

It was her favorite trip, she told me—that's what she always said, and I always loved to hear it.

We lost track of time, and we were out there past dark, exploring the cave, climbing the rocks, building stone symbols in the dirt, and collecting gems in the washouts. Sierra found her first arrowhead that day. She dug it up with her hands. She held it up to me and laughed with delight. There was mud on her hands, there were thistles in her hair, there were pebbles sticking to the skin of her knees. I was in love.

This memory, I realize, is Lorac's gift to me.

Leaving the store and its characters behind for a while, Jennifer Morse takes to the trail.

CHAPTER ELEVEN

Minnesota Smith

its time the truth be told. it cant hurt my creation. i ,..matthewski,..
made minnesota smith. i breathed life into him like god did us. without
the creator,.. there can be no created. i made minnesota smith out of a
void. to fill a need. a sociatle need.you needed a scapegoat to vent your
destructive negetivisms. minnesota smith came into being to acheive
just such venting. lest the time space continnium crap out.now ,.. more
than ever,.. inventers like me,.. will create such things. as the end draws
ni.beware yall,....the end surly commeth . . . .   —mweinstone

[POSTED ON WWW.WHITEBLAZE.NET]

Whiteblaze.net is one of the most popular Internet community discussion forums for
the Appalachian Trail. For A.T. hikers, Whiteblaze is the equivalent of Facebook,
Twitter, or YouTube—a meeting place for staying in touch with friends or arguing
with enemies, but also an instant generator of fads, scandals, and small-time
celebrities. One of the stars of Whiteblaze, a man who has stretched his fame
beyond the usual fifteen minutes, is Minnesota Smith. I've never seen a legend
rise from the dust of this trail so quickly. When I first meet him, he declares that
he's already famous. He greets me at the door. "Hi, my name is Luke; they call
me Minnesota Smith," he says. "You probably know me. I have over thirty-five
hundred postings on Whiteblaze."

I see before me an orange kerchief, a hat, some glasses, a paunch, and
a mess of tangled fabrics bent under an enormous, overloaded pack. I can't tell
where Minnesota Smith's voice is coming from.

"Really? Wow," I say. "That is a lot of typing."

I get a look at him as the outer layers come off. A pale, doughy man emerges, like a newly hatched grub. Luke is in his early forties. His head is as bald and shiny as a bowling ball on top, but shaggy with blond hair at the sides and back. Large, plastic-frame glasses with thick lenses hang lopsided on his pudgy face. A crust of sunscreen covers his nose, and white gloves cover his hands.

From his forward way of speaking and from the smirk on his face, it is clear that this man is intelligent and yet socially graceless, and satisfied with himself on both counts. In grade school he would have been that kid who was always getting slammed against his locker. His voice is a low, slow monotone, and at times his sentences seem to lack all inflection, and they definitely lack punctuation.

"Yes it is a lot of typing," he says. "I want you to go through my pack—I don't know of anything that I could possibly get rid of at this point but would like to see what you have to say—I have studied this for a long time and have read quite a lot on hiking the Appalachian Trail and have met some people who have actually done it before and talked to them and they helped me a little. You come highly recommended from people on all the forums—I have a special diet and need certain foods and ointments—I'm quite sensitive to the sun so I need a lot of protective clothes. Where do you want me to spread my stuff out? It's all down in the hostel; can we do it down there? I have a two-man tent—I know you're not going to like that—I made my own alcohol stove—I'll show it to you; which alcohol stove do you like? Did you ever see—"

The diatribe goes on and on. Eventually I lose track of what he's saying. My mind just shuts him out, as if he's an AM radio playing in the next room. Why is this man in front of me now? There is no opportunity to interrupt and no hope of a rescue. The rest of the staff, fearing that I'll try to hand Minnesota off, have all decided that they're busy with something that needs immediate attention. Buddy restocks candy bars. Nate goes to the shelf where we keep coffee mugs and turns them, one at a time, so that their handles all point in the same direction.

Minnesota's next act is to commence a hacking noise at the back of his throat, as if all those lost periods and commas had been building in his esophagus and are screaming to come out. I seize the opportunity to speak.

"I think an alcohol stove is a good choice for some people, but it's not—"

"Well—*hurk, hurk*—which fuels do you use? Denatured Heet? *Hurk, hurk.* Or isopropyl alcohol?"

"Denatured, of course," I say with certainty.

"That's good. Let me show you why. Give me that piece of paper." He pulls a pen from his shirt pocket and takes away my receipt from the morning beverage delivery. After diagramming the molecular structure for denatured, methanol, and isopropyl alcohol, he cruises through a ten-minute chemistry lecture. He talks about which elements the various fuel alcohols have in common and finally finishes with: "and anyone can see that it's the two-part carbon that makes denatured a better fuel for cooking."

"I really should have listened more in class," I say. I ask him if he's a chemical engineer.

"No, I am a geologist," he replies. "For the past several years I have worked on oil rigs, compiling subsurface reports that tell them where to stick the drill and when to change the damn thing—a broken drill bit could cost them upwards of twenty to thirty thousand dollars—you see, I am one of only a few working on oil rigs that holds three master's degrees in geosciences—"

"What made you decide to hike the Appalachian Trail?"

Here at last he pauses, but just for a moment—frowning and swallowing, irritated at having been interrupted in the middle of rattling off his educational background. His answer is ready, but he has to change gears to call it up.

"I am looking for a wife," he says, and swivels his eyes from side to side, looking. "Not just anyone will do. She can't be older than twenty-seven because that is the best age for childbearing."

Minnesota tells me he's heard of our shakedown service and he's looking forward to making use of it. He says he's looking forward to showing off his gear.

"Should be fun," I say. "The shop's closing in about an hour, so we'll have to do this later. I'll meet you down in the hostel in about an hour and a half."

"Perfect; that would be good and give me time to organize my stuff," he says. "You should have four drop boxes of food and water for me here. Where can I pick that up? Do you have any boot driers in the hostel?"

"No, we don't have boot driers, and yes, I know exactly where your boxes are. I'll get them for you."

So that's who he is, I think: he's the man who shipped three cases of water to himself in care of the store—each case containing four one-gallon jugs—and another thirty pounds of food. I was expecting him to show up with a mule. The stuff has all been sitting in the back room for more than a month.

It takes three more hikers to get his payload down to the hostel. I carry my case quietly. I don't want to ask about the water for fear that a hydrology lesson will ensue.

I'm no good at picking finishers, but the odds didn't look good. He's green fer sure and thats his smallest worry. But he is trying and if there is anyone that a thruhike would do wonders for, it is this man. I hope he ends up on Katahdin- a new man.   —Nean

[POSTED ON WWW.WHITEBLAZE.NET]

The next hour moves slowly. The last hikers of the day are coming in from Gooch Gap Shelter, fourteen miles away. Food and a warm place to sleep are their main concerns.

Nate volunteers to close everything up and suggests that I go down and get started with Luke. Felicity is finishing a shakedown with a kid in the back. "You sure?" I say.

"Oh, yeah," he says. "Got you covered. Unless Felicity would rather—"

"No, that's all right," Felicity shouts from the back. "Still finishing up here."

"So I guess we'll just let you take care of the famous Minnesota Smith, Winton."

"Nate, where is Alpine?"

"That reminds me," Nate says. "He needs your help. He's on the porch with some woman and had a question for you."

"I'll check on him and head down to the hostel. See you in the morning."

I walk out on the front porch, and Alpine grabs me, beyond earshot of his customer. "Hey, boss, listen. This woman needs some tough love. She has a forty-degree flannel bag, all cotton clothing except for the five bras she's packing, and one of those spring-loaded self-poppy-up tents. She said she bought it on the Home Shopping Network."

"Why is she out here?"

"She said that she wanted to lose some weight, get back in shape, and hiking to Maine was something that she always wanted to do."

"What's her name?"

"She is going by Cozy."

I look over Alpine's shoulder and see Cozy putting on lipstick while using her cell phone as a mirror. Cozy is a short, busty, heavy-bodied brunette, well kept with a tender face. I guess late twenties. She is in unusually high spirits for someone so poorly equipped. When I walk over, she closes the cell phone and purses her lips to even out her lipstick.

"Cozy, has Alpine managed to help you out a little?"

"Yes, and thank y'all so much," she says. "I know that I want that tent, but can't afford the sleeping bag right now. I could do some work around here if you like?"

Here are some clues: He likes to recline on the store's roof. He carries a flute. He has a beard. His trail name starts with B.

"Well, we are pretty well covered."

"I can do that too," she says with a winsome smile.

Alpine and I turn to one another in an attempt to verify our interpretation. Cozy apparently is having trouble figuring out just who is whose customer here.

"Is there by chance a Waffle House around here?" she asks.

I tell her that the closest Waffle House is probably the one in Gainesville, a Georgia town best known for being on Lake Lanier, about an hour away. "Why? Are you hungry?"

"No. I used to work for Waffle House, and once you've been with the company for over a year, you can pick up any shift at any of their stores in the country."

"No kidding?" Alpine says. "Kind of like an exchange program."

"Yes. You wouldn't know if the one in Gainesville is near a truck stop?"

Alpine and I exchange another look. I ask her if that would really matter.

She says, "Totally! I can make better tips if it's near a truck stop. Plus, if I can pull a few favors, I can get an extra couple hundred in a night."

"Well, ma'am, we like to consider ourselves a full-service shop," Alpine says.

"You're in capable hands here, ma'am," I say. "There isn't a person better trained than my friend Alpine here for helping someone get what they need. I have a hiker in the hostel that needs my help with a pack."

Alpine hands Cozy the keys to his Rodeo, invites her to climb in and pick out a CD for the ride to Waffle House, and says he'll join her after a word with me.

"You want a free piece of advice, Sergeant Ingram? Just give her a ride to the Waffle House."

"I think you might be right, boss."

"You're thinking a couple things."

He grins. "Actually, I'm sort of curious about this girl named Jennifer you hired that I keep hearing about. I hear she is cute."

"Stand down, sergeant," I warn him. "She's too smart for you. Plus, she has a boyfriend. His name is John."

The fact is that it had crossed my mind the moment I heard that Alpine was headed back to the mountain that these two would be perfect for each other. We had known Jennifer Morse for a few years, but hired her only recently to work a few days a week. They wouldn't be able to miss each other for long.

Jennifer is a young, beautiful, magnetic personality who says she loves everyone "in a peace-and-joy, seventies kind of way." She has a tremendous appetite for conversation: she'll start up a talk with anyone and hangs onto your every word as if yours were the most interesting tale she's ever heard. Her strength and her weakness is that she wants to be the savior of all wounded birds.

Her generosity of spirit, her willingness as a listener, and her natural curiosity have made her at times the victim of other people's sicknesses and needs. The needs of John, her on-and-off boyfriend, could be violently demanding. She isn't very happy with John. I'll let Alpine find that out for himself.

John is handsome and slim, with long, saddle-brown hair, and he's strong, from wielding a hammer in a construction job for eight hours a day. With his mouth closed, he exudes confidence and intelligence, but at heart he is a frightened, distrustful man. He takes out his pains and insecurities on Jennifer. We have heard of him smashing windows, shoving her into walls, and once breaking her hand with a wild swing of a hammer. When I imagine Jennifer meeting Alpine, I imagine a romantic rescue. Master Sergeant Ingram could be her hero.

"How long has she been with John?" Alpine asks.

"Awhile. You'll meet her soon enough," I say. "So I guess things didn't work out with you and your wife. Remember her?"

"No, they didn't work out. We ended up getting a divorce. The truth is, I am done with women for a while." When he says this, I can see that he wants to believe it. "After the divorce, I don't think I want to get involved. I just want to take it slow and enjoy life."

Across the lot, the Rodeo starts up, its lights come on, the stereo blares Lynyrd Skynyrd, and the horn honks twice.

"Time me," he says. "Just a ride to the Waffle House. I'm telling you." (It turns out that Alpine does keep this promise.)

"There's a man back there in the hostel who's looking for a wife on the Trail, you know," I say.

> i heard he is carrying 6 liters of water an was arguing with other hikers when they told him hed did not need 6 liters of water at a time.the guy is going to hurt himself,i calculated the odds 500 to 1,he will not make it —neo

Minnesota Smith has his gear lined up on a twenty-foot stretch of floor along the north side of the hostel. The room is silent when I walk in—or rather, everybody is silent except Luke, aka Minnesota Smith, who is sitting on the couch behind his gear and declaiming, from a legal-size piece of paper, what sounds like a prayer. Several hikers are standing in front of the gear, lined up like tourists who have paid admission to inspect some menagerie of oddities. I quietly close the door behind me, trying not to disturb the sacred moment. Luke goes on with the recitation in a raised voice, warbling with artificial emotion:

> *This is the Law of the Yukon, that only the Strong shall thrive;*
> *That surely the Weak shall perish, and only the Fit survive.*
> *Dissolute, damned and despairful, crippled and palsied and slain,*
> *This is the Will of the Yukon, — Lo, how she makes it plain!*

"And that my friends is 'The Law of the Yukon!' " Luke concludes. He looks up and sees me standing next to the door.

"Winton, you missed it. I was just reading the words of the great Robert Service. I will get you a copy for the wall here in the hostel. The hikers love it when I read it."

Actually, the hikers are exhausted and quiet. Many of them have slept right through the oration.

"I caught the tail end of it, and from what I heard it sounded great. What was that one line—'crippled?' "

" 'Crippled and palsied and slain,' " he quotes approvingly.

"Great. Really motivational," I say. "Should we get started with the surgery?"

The hikers who have lined up like tourists step back from the gear, giving me full access to the equipment on the floor. I set the parameters with Luke so that he knows exactly what is going to happen over the next hour.

"Luke, I am going to go through each one of these sections of gear: clothing, water, cooking, first aid, personal, miscellaneous, tent, and sleep system. I am going to pull things to the side that you will not agree with. Please, let me just pull them aside, and if you want to sneak them back in later, then fine. If I know something that will work differently, then I will tell you about it. If you want to integrate my advice into your system, great. If you don't, you will not hurt my feelings. The goal is to make you lighter, more efficient, and safe. Do you understand?"

Luke nods his head happily. He's got nothing to hide; in fact he's ready to show it all off and teach me a thing or two about hiking. He's like a patient with plans to beat his doctor in an arm-wrestling match.

"First let's start with clothing. . . ."

> I don't care if MS is a hiking machine, he's still an idiot. HYOH [Hike your own hike], MS, and thank goodness you can't keep me from hiking mine.
> —Marta

Over the next hour and half we go through seventy-five pounds of gear. Beyond what a normal hiker would wear, Luke carries town clothes and sleep clothes, a "date night" shirt and a set of emergency "never get wet" clothes vacuum-sealed in plastic. His plans for wilderness courtship are very serious, and he knows he has to be fully prepared if he wants to find a mate under the twenty-seven-year age limit. He carries enough underwear to last ten days.

He has one gas stove and two alcohol stoves. He says that he is thinking of getting rid of one of the alcohol stoves, but is still trying to decide which one he likes better. His water system is more like a water-treatment plant: several Nalgene bottles, plastic water tanks, panty hose, chlorine drops, gravity filter, pump filter, special filter straws. His fear of creek water is manic, and he is unwilling to part with anything that has to do with filtering water, with the exception of one Nalgene bottle (the smallest one). He has arranged to have several hundred gallons of water shipped to him along the Trail in resupply boxes, but he is beginning to think, sadly, that he will have to abandon that plan because of the cost. His first aid and personal kit is chock-full of razors, shaving cream, protective skin ointments, and bacteria-fighting scrubs. He insists that it is no use for me to even go through it, because he has already taken out a whole pound of stuff that he is going to send home.

As for food—besides a typical collection of noodles and oatmeal, Luke carries cans of asparagus, corn, peaches, kidney beans, and soup, and multiple bags of dried squid, seaweed, minnows, and fruitcake. And he carries nine rolls of toilet paper.

"Luke, why do you have nine rolls of toilet paper and two rolls of paper towels?"

"I know," he says. "I should have taken out the cardboard rolls in the middle."

"How many rolls did you start with?"

"I started with sixteen rolls. I go through about a roll per day."

"Holy crap. That must be enough toilet paper to blanket every mile from here back to Springer. What is wrong with you, man?"

"I eat a lot of fiber. It's the only way that I get enough nourishment along the Trail."

"Well, that certainly helps to explain the few pounds of ointment you have in the first-aid kit. I hope the future Mrs. Minnesota Smith is into raisin bran."

I pull four rolls of toilet paper to the side, leaving him with five, and tell him that it is only four days to the next town, so the extra roll is just for insurance.

At long last, I tell him, "I have done about as much as I can do, Luke. The decisions are now up to you. But you may want to consider one last thing."

"What would that be?"

"The grizzly spray that you're hiding behind your back. You could blind yourself."

"It's not for bears, it's for dogs," he says. "I can't stand them. They shouldn't even be allowed on the Trail. They can ruin the experience for me and everybody else."

"Luke, some people can ruin the experience for everybody else."

A hiker named Stewmeat who I thought was asleep in the corner—asleep with his dog tied up outside—says, "You spray my dog with that shit, and you'll find yourself tied naked to a tree with your balls marinating in it. How's that for the Law of the goddamned Yukon?"

Minnesota Smith reluctantly hands over the spray, and I toss it into the small pile of stuff to send home.

"Luke, it's late and I have an early day in the morning," I say. "I would love to hang out and talk with you more, but you have a lot to think about, and I need some sleep. I'll see you in the morning."

"What time do you open?"

"Eight-thirty."

"I am going to take a zero," he says, meaning in hiker-speak that he would have a nonhiking day. "My mom is coming up from Atlanta in the morning to bring me a few things, and I want you to meet her."

"Your mom?"

"Yes, she is my support group for the Trail."

"What the hell else do you need?"

"I'm running out of underwear. She's bringing another couple of pairs."

"I'll be here for you, Luke. Get some sleep."

the funny thing is that MS's best thread is when he was off the computer.

—Tha Wookie

[POSTED ON WWW.WHITEBLAZE.NET]

Now, I still can't help but think that beneath the exterior of this man lives a peaceful, happy soul, almost ready and planning—tomorrow, next month, next year—to get out. Minnesota's condescending attitude and his distrust of other people's ideas would have taken years to develop. The know-it-all attitude, the bullying nerdiness, were what was left of a teenage defense mechanism. He was using his intelligence as a weapon against loneliness. Men like him need this trail, for the healing it can give; and the Trail needed him, for the color.

After a few days, Luke moved through. During his stay he managed to piss off most of the people here, women more than men; a few were intrigued, and others he just left confused. At one point, Alpine was ready to kick him out, and several people were refusing to stay in the hostel as long as he was there.

I learned more about Minnesota Smith later on Whiteblaze, where a thread that followed Minnesota Smith's progress eventually became, and remains, one of the longest discussion topics in the near-decade-long history of the Web site. Just as he had told me, he was a celebrity in that online community, where for a year prior to his hike he had aired his pointed views on every subject from birth control, child-rearing, and the role of women in society to energy policy, illegal immigration, and dog-leashing laws. Occasionally he wrote about hiking, too, but his thoughts on that subject were no better received than the others. When the members of the cyber-hiker community weren't deriding him as a sexist reactionary, they were complaining that his political views had no business anyway on a site about hiking the Appalachian Trail; when he did write about hiking the Appalachian Trail, they jeered at him because he had never done it. He had an opinion on everything, and he could be provoked into five hundred or more half-crazy words by anyone, anytime, on anything. He was the pet monster that every blog needs.

When at last he set out on his thru-hike, it was soon documented that he was doing everything wrong. He was too fat. He was too slow. He was carrying too much. Whiteblaze users formed betting pools, not only to wager against Minnesota Smith's reaching Katahdin, but even to lay odds on which part of his body (bad knee, bad ankle, bad skin, bad intestine) would give out first. For the first month or two of his trip, he was scorned and chastised on nearly every A.T. forum in existence.

But while the bloggers babbled, Minnesota Smith kept walking, and with every step, he earned respect. The thread that began as a betting book on his chances of failure eventually became the most remarkable fan club of its kind on the Internet. A number of celebrated hikers—including Lone Wolf, Baltimore Jack, Tin Man, AWOL, and many others—used the thread to invite him into their homes. They fed him, gave him a place to sleep, and went back online to confirm his existence and describe their meetings with him.

One dedicated Whiteblazer, Dances with Mice, was Minnesota Smith's beat reporter; another, Matthew "Matthewski" Weinstone, was his poet laureate. While Dances with Mice kept the site refreshed with the most up-to-date information available on Minnesota's progress, Matthewski wrote short, cryptic odes to him in the style of Jack Kerouac. The thread filled up with the encouragements of Whiteblazers who said they had disagreed with Minnesota Smith, argued with him, been insulted by him, or found him repulsive and still did, and yet they wished him success on the Trail. As whole weeks went by without an unkind word in cyberspace from Minnesota Smith, Whiteblazers began to wonder about the power of a thru-hike to change a man's heart. And although the reports coming off the Trail promised Whiteblazers that he was as obnoxious and bizarre as ever, he hiked all the way until the middle of April before he made another sharp-worded post to the site: that was when he warned someone not to call him "Minny."

The last call I got from him during his hike was when he was in Hanover, New Hampshire, hanging out with Baltimore Jack. His plan was to skip north 140 miles to give himself a bigger window of time to make Katahdin before it closed on October 15. He would then flip back down, finish the part he missed, and be done before the end of November.

The next time I heard from him was through a package that arrived sometime before Christmas. Inside were two boot driers, a framed copy of "The Law of the Yukon," and a picture of him on top of Katahdin. A note scribbled on the back read:

THRU COMPLETED, PS: DROP THE OSPREY IN FAVOR OF GREGORY PACKS, PLEASE, THANKS

MINNESOTA SMITH, APPALACHIAN TRAIL THRU-HIKE ATOP OF MOUNT KATAHDIN—MAINE READING *LAW OF YUKON* POEM BY ROBERT SERVICE.

Pirate, ready for the trail, tries out some new shades.

CHAPTER TWELVE
The Foot

It's not just the shade and seclusion of the woods that makes the southern Appalachians a natural refuge for outlaws. It's something deep in the character of the local people, the rural distrustfulness—of "big government" in general, and of cops, judges, and lawyers in particular—that runs in their blood. For the man on the run, getting help and sympathy in these woods is a question of marketing. If he can bill himself as a modern Robin Hood—an underdog free spirit battling the corrupt, overreaching forces of taxation—he'll find some friends out here. The most famous and most lovable outlaws were the legends of the bootlegging business. While mythical moonshine runners were memorialized in *Thunder Road, Deliverance,* and *The Dukes of Hazzard,* the real ones, including Junior Johnson of NASCAR fame, hid in these mountains for years, distributing tax-free liquor and teaching people how to drive like maniacs.

Today, the right phone call can still turn up a little white lightning for a special occasion, but the old rivers of moonshine have mostly dried up, and the fugitives aren't what they used to be, either. The most notorious of recent years was the terrorist Eric Robert Rudolph, who bombed Atlanta's Olympic Park during the 1996 Olympics. He later went into hiding in the western North Carolina (and possibly North Georgia) woods after he bombed a gay bar in Atlanta and abortion clinics in Georgia and Alabama. He had killed 2 people and injured more than 120 when, in 1998, the FBI put him on its Ten Most Wanted list and tracked him into the woods.

When I came to Mountain Crossings, in 2001, Rudolph was still on the loose. Whenever his apparent trail passed close to our nearby town of Blairsville, the pack of FBI agents who followed it would come to the store and try to get information from the hikers. The FBI men—well dressed, clean shaven, and smartly equipped—stuck out like Oreos in orange juice, and they didn't like us. They thought we were Rudolph's friends. Now, there was a small and loud super-redneck minority in the area that actually supported Rudolph's vague crusade against abortion, homosexuality, and globalization. (He was a white supremacist, too, just for good measure.) Somebody without much in the way of conscience made a few bucks selling "Run Rudolph Run" T-shirts.

The press, meanwhile, loved telling the story of the savage natives protecting one of their own from the FBI. Once, it was reported that Rudolph had come through Mountain Crossings and had even stopped in to get a canned drink and a chocolate bar. We could not confirm or deny that the man had come to our store. He would have been a thin white man with a shaggy beard, covered in dirt and smelling awful—like half of the customers in the store. One reporter wanted to know if I could show her some of the bugs I thought he was eating, and another wanted to know if I thought Rudolph really had a chance against all the wild animals—such as bears, cougars, and coyotes. I told her I was afraid he did have a chance against Georgia's cougars.

Most of us wanted to help (certainly in educating reporters about how many decades it had been since anyone had seen a wild cougar in North Georgia). We just didn't know anything. There was a very simple reason we didn't know anything—the woods are big, the Trail is small—but we had trouble explaining this to the FBI. They were city men who thought of the size of a place in terms of population rather than square miles, and they kept expecting to find him under somebody's bed, even when all a citizen had to do to get a million-dollar reward was to give information that would "lead" to Rudolph's arrest. I took a shot at that reward. I gave an agent some tips on blending in with the hiker community: grow a beard, wear less black, smoke some grass, put a few bumper stickers on the Town Car, I said, and maybe you'll crack the case. He was not amused. Eventually Rudolph's trail turned north, and the FBI moved away from Mountain Crossings. Until that dog arrives. . . .

Today I walk out of the house and into the breezeway with Sky by my side and hear Billy hollering in the backyard.

"Give me that! Give it to me!"

Billy is leaning against the stone wall about twenty feet from the breezeway and playing what appears to be a friendly game of tug-of-war with an old hound that keeps a firm grip with its jaws on an old leather boot. Sky, who has always found certain dog behaviors beneath her, sighs and goes to find a place to sit. She stations herself a few paces away—close enough to protect us if the hound should turn violent, far enough away to show the hound that she will not play any game that involves tugging at something with her mouth.

I've never seen this hound before, and I wasn't expecting to see Billy. I tell him I thought he was out hiking.

"I got back this morning. Camped a mile back at Bull Gap last night," he says quickly. "Would you mind giving me a hand here?"

"I hope you didn't drag that dog back with you. If you did, he is your problem. That would be the third in a month. Don't tell me you fed him."

"I didn't feed him! Now would you shut up and help me get this damn boot out of his mouth?" Billy shouts, jerking at the boot. The old hound digs in and pulls all his weight back on his haunches, flattening his back and growling happily.

"What do you want me to do, exactly? Goose him?"

"Why not? Give it a try. But do something!"

I say, "Release!"

The dog immediately releases the boot into Billy's hand, causing him to fall against the stone wall. "Well, that wasn't so hard." He chuckles.

"It's a coon dog or squirrel dog. It's trained to sniff 'em, kill 'em, and bring 'em back to the pickup truck or something. What are you going to do with this dog?"

"Look at this boot."

"Yeah. It's an old Wolverine work boot. I don't want it."

"No," Billy says. "Look at this boot! There is a foot still in it!"

I look over, and Billy turns the boot toward me so I can see inside. In a mess of dry leaves and dirt, I make out what can only be bones. "Damn, Billy. Where do you think he found it?"

"I don't know. I spent the night at Bull Gap. The dog showed up there last night, but he didn't have a boot in his mouth. He showed up again about thirty minutes ago as I was putting on my pack and had this damn boot, and he hasn't let it out of his mouth since."

"Bumblefoot, I know you can walk these woods with your eyes closed. Why don't you try it sometime? Don't you know dead people in the woods is bad for business?"

"Tell that to the dog, Winton," he says. "I told him I had a feeling that it didn't belong to him."

Billy carries the boot up to the balcony and carefully lays it on one of the picnic tables. He pauses a moment and takes a bashful look around, then sits down at the table, slouching so as to stare at the boot eye to eye. He looks as if he wants to ask it a question. I bring the cordless phone from the shop out to the balcony and dial 911.

"What's your emergency, please?"

"We found a boot on the Trail," I say. "No. That's not it. I mean, we found this boot—"

"Sir, I wouldn't consider that an emergency."

"No, no, listen—we found a boot with a foot in it."

"Sir, I am wearing a boot with a foot in it right now. Sir, do you realize that it's a crime to prank-call a—"

"We found a boot with a foot in it and nothing else in it."

"Not even the whole foot," Billy says. "Just the bones."

"Not even a foot, just the bones," I say.

"Who is this? Sir, what is your name?"

"This is Winton, owner of Mountain Crossings, and I have found, or rather, a dog brought to me, a boot, with the skeleton of a human foot still in the damn thing!"

"Do you know who it belongs to, sir?"

"No ma'am, I do not. Do you know anybody who's missing one?"

"We'll send an officer up."

After about twenty minutes, a sheriff's car pulls into the parking lot. A young officer leaps out with clipboard in hand. He's a short and skinny man who has to make the most of what he's got. For height, he holds himself up as straight as he can; for bulk, he's got a Kevlar vest and a belt buckle the size of a license plate, but an extraordinary amount of him is mustache. We greet Officer Mustache at the top of the stairs and take him to the boot.

"The boot's over here," Billy says importantly, like a secretary showing us in to the boss's office. The boot sits up on the picnic table, looking impressive and heavy. Officer Mustache gives the boot some room while he examines it. He's careful not to touch it with his hands. He has to belly up to the picnic table and lean over, all five-foot-five of him, as far as he can, to see inside. Then, after he has picked and poked at the boot with his pen for a few minutes—tilting it up, then letting it settle, listening to the chalky rattle of the contents—he proclaims, "Yep, I think you are right. That looks like a boot with a foot stuck in there. Let me make a call, and I'll be right back to get some more information. Don't let anybody touch that boot."

Billy moves over to the boot and calls out: "Sir, does that mean you just deputized me?"

"Come on, Deputy Bumblefoot," I say. "This is serious."

Billy and I stand around counting minutes, looking at the boot every now and then, making sure it's comfortable, waiting for the officer to return. The boot sits quietly a little while, and then it starts whispering to us, working on us, reminding us of what it really is: a vessel containing pieces of a dead man. Not knowing who the dead man was, we'd found it easy at first to make the boot into a prop, a gag. Now the same ignorance makes us feel irresponsible and shabby. You have to know somebody and be his friend to have the right to tease him. We don't know who's in that boot. Billy goes into the store and brings out two coffees and one Snickers bar. We talk to break up the tension.

"You didn't bring me a Snickers?"

"Thought you were a vegetarian," he says through a sticky mouthful.

Officer Mustache returns and takes another look at the boot. "Didn't one of you find a body over at Jarrard Gap a few months ago?"

"Yes, that would be me, sir," I tell him. "I found the campsite, looked for the person, but you guys found the body. His name was Earthworm."

"Earthworm?"

"I don't know his real name."

It had been six months before. I was on a ten-mile run from Woody Gap and came across a campsite about five miles in at Jarrard Gap. I was going to pass by, but I noticed that the rain fly was not on the tent. It had been raining for the past twelve hours.

I stopped and discovered a tent full of water, a soaked sleeping bag, an unopened pack of cigarettes, and a Bible with "Earthworm" penned inside. I recognized the name of a thin, gawky man who came through the store two or three times a year; he had signed the guestbook in the same childish scrawl. He was called Earthworm for his skinny, wormy build. I remembered that he was a drinker, but never a violent one. He had told us that he was carrying the Bible because he wanted to learn more about it. "Figure I'll give just about all of the religions a chance, then pick out the one that works for me," he said. "I'm starting with the Bible because it's the easiest one to find in English." That was the extent of Earthworm's proselytizing. We had seen him at the store, alive and bizarre, less than a week before I came across his campsite.

His food bag was strangely hung about four feet from the ground, and his JanSport external-frame pack was leaning against a tree. I rummaged through the pack and found a Home Depot receipt, a cell phone, and half-empty bottles of vodka and Percodan. I looked around the perimeter and called out for Earthworm for about fifteen minutes. I couldn't get a cell signal there, but I knew that I could get one on top of Blood Mountain, so I kept running. At the top of the mountain, I called the store.

In the end, Earthworm was found. He had fallen thirty feet from a tree and landed on his head. No one could figure out why he had been in the tree. He wasn't a hunter, and he had been known to enjoy his alcohol and painkillers just as much on solid ground as anywhere else. We missed Earthworm and the erratic chatter he brought to the store. He was one of those strange characters that you couldn't help but like. At Mountain Crossings we had a high tolerance for strange.

Officer Mustache leads Billy aside with his notepad and pen and questions him for the next ten minutes. Billy repeats the story he told me at the back of the breezeway. Within an hour, the parking lot is filling up with the sheriff, more deputies, rescue teams, marked and unmarked police cars. Then the men in the black cars, the black sunglasses, the black suits start showing up. One group of them strips out of their suits right there in the lot, changing into nylon pants, black combat boots, and jungle vests with large yellow letters embroidered on the back: GBI, for the Georgia Bureau of Investigation.

"Billy, do you have any idea why the GBI are here?"

"Not a clue. And the FBI just pulled in."

Lawmen keep coming in. They get out of their cars and stand around in small groups grumbling secretly, holding their hands over their mouths like baseball players congregating on the pitching mound. No one says a word to us during this muster, so we do our best to open the store and do some business. The boot now has an appointed armed guard. The picnic table gets cordoned off with yellow crime scene tape.

After about half an hour, we see Officer Mustache talking on the stairs with a man in an FBI battle vest. The officer looks up and points his finger in our direction. He introduces me and Billy, and Mr. FBI reaches out and shakes our hands.

The agent asks Billy: "You think you can get that dog of yours to follow you back into the woods to the place where you stayed last night?"

"It's not my dog," Billy says with an air of indignation. "Though I did have an old hound a long time ago, and come to think of it, he was always carrying off people's shoes—"

"Billy, do you think you could get that dog, whoever the hell's dog that is, to go back to where your campsite was last night?" says Mr. FBI.

"Yes, sir! Let me grab a leash and get some more beef jerky."

I glare at Billy and try to catch him directly in the eye so he can read my thoughts: You told me you didn't feed that dog.

The FBI agent pulls Billy to one side and talks with him in private. They spend a few minutes together, and then Billy steps into the shop to grab a leash from the shelf and some beef jerky.

"I owe you for some beef jerky and two Snickers bars," he says. "You'll have to put it on my tab. I'm a deputy today."

"Come on, Billy. Who are they looking for?"

"Rudolph. They think it could be Rudolph. They're hoping this boot is the biggest thing left of him."

"Damn. I forgot about that guy. Of course."

"Gotta run. Rover and I are going for a hike," Billy says, whistling to his new four-footed companion. "See you in a few hours."

A team of eight heads out through the breezeway and up the Trail, with Billy and the dog leading the way. As they're leaving, Buddy's burgundy Chevy Astro van goes crawling through the lot, looking for a space in the sea of government vehicles, which are parked in various cockeyed directions. (It makes sense to me when I think about it: if you work for the FBI, you can park as badly as you want to.) After a few minutes, Buddy gives up and simply stops in the middle of the lot, jams into park, and steps out of the car yelling to no one in particular: "You people! Didn't your daddy teach you how to park?!"

A few officers turn their heads, but no one is really listening.

"What the hell is going on?" Buddy asks me when he gets inside. "No one out there would even talk to me."

"This morning a dog brought us a boot with skeletal remains of a foot still in it, and they think it may be Rudolph."

"A dog? A boot with a—"

"Yes. It's long story. Billy's out with them now at Bull Gap trying to help them find the rest of the guy."

"Bull Gap? That's not Rudolph—it's Hobbs!"

I draw a blank.

"Hobbs!" Buddy says. "Remember? That abandoned campsite that Nate found up there a couple of years ago?"

Yes. Of course. "That was just before my time," I say. "But yeah, I've heard you guys talking about it so many times. They never found a body—"

"We had two Polaroids of the guy," Buddy says. "One was a group shot with other hikers, and another was a head shot that we put in the thru-hiker album. The police took one of them, plus about eighty pounds of camping gear that Nate dragged out of the woods."

I ask Buddy, "You think you could find that other photo?"

"I know exactly where it is. I'll grab it for you."

The whole Hobbs episode was two winters earlier, just before I bought the store. I knew the story well, though, because Nate had been telling it for some time as a spook story: the tale of the abandoned campsite. "I had actually seen Hobbs's campsite once before and ignored it," Nate would say as we sat around a fire. "Everything looked normal. But then I go past it again, a week later, and it doesn't look so normal anymore."

When Nate checked inside the tent, he found a wet sleeping bag, a journal, two books, and some trash that looked as if it had been dragged in by small animals. When Nate reported the find to the sheriff's office, he learned that the sheriff had no missing-person report for a hiker. The officers asked him to gather the equipment in plastic bags, and they would come and pick it up a few days later.

"Hobbs was packing cheap gear, and you know it's not uncommon for people to abandon cheap gear on the Trail," Nate said. "And his journal was full of stuff about 'demons circling my head' and 'people's voices in the air all the time.' We concluded that the guy's hearing voices; he freaked out. One of the voices in his head ordered him to walk off the Trail and leave everything behind."

The store keeps photographs and logbooks of hikers passing through; the logbooks go back twenty years. After the Polaroid of Hobbs was given to law enforcement, it took a few more weeks and a couple of phone calls to the sheriff's department to get the deputies to pick up the gear. Dorothy Hansen, the owner of Mountain Crossings at that time, located a sister of Hobbs's in Philadelphia. The sister said that she didn't know or much care where Hobbs was and that no one in the family was looking for him. "He goes out all the time, and we have no idea where he's going. He does this all the time."

How can you be missing if no one is looking for you?

Two months after that, the sister called the sheriff to see if Hobbs had shown up. He hadn't. A missing-person report was filed. No one had come forward with any news about Hobbs in all that time. Until the dog, today.

Outside, several officers are still in the parking lot, leaning against cars, writing in notebooks, and talking on cell phones. The guardian of the boot is still perched on the balcony with the dead man's foot. Officer Mustache is climbing the stairs and headed my way. Buddy steps outside with Polaroid in hand and says to me, "Here you go, boss. That's him in the middle."

"Officer, I think this is the man you are looking for," I say. "We call him Hobbs, and down at the station, tucked away in some box with some old camping equipment, you should have a head shot of the guy. The folks who owned this place before me gave it to you about two years ago. See his feet? There's the old tan Wolverine boots, sir."

Glancing at the photograph as I hand it over, I feel as though I'm seeing it for the first time. This man Hobbs was a ghost once; he is very real to me now. There he is, the man in the boot: midforties, lanky, clean shaven. Bald, but letting his curly hair grow wild at the back and sides, for compensation perhaps. Round wire frames, behind which his eyes seem to be retreating, getting hollower every year. A solitary, intellectual man, carrying a sadness with him. As old as he'll ever be.

Seeing the Polaroid takes the wind out of the officer's sails. His shoulders drop as he studies the picture. He doesn't say anything—simply turns and walks away, still staring at the photograph in his hand as he takes it down to the officers in the parking lot. I watch as the scrawny young deputy shows the picture to his commander in the parking lot. A circle of officers begins to form around the photograph. Their reactions to the photo are the same:

shoulders dropped, hands thrown up, feet stamped. A few of them look down at their guns with sadness. They'd been hoping to shoot someone today.

Most of the FBI and GBI depart within an hour of the appearance of Buddy's Polaroid, leaving only the local police and rescue. By evening, the ordeal is coming to a close. Billy is back and has resumed his seat on the roof with his flute. Buddy is back at the register. The word is out as to why every cop in Union County has been in our parking lot, and even the hikers who smell most conspicuously of marijuana are beginning to relax. I am trying to help a woman with some infected blisters when Officer Mustache comes back for a last word.

"Excuse me, Mr. Porter—can I speak to you for a moment?"

His tone is more subdued than before, and he lets his Southern accent come through more warmly now. He explains that they've found scraps of a shirt matching the color of the shirt Hobbs wears in the picture. "More bones, too," he says, "all over the place. The coyotes and bears have scattered him all over the forest. You could have people bringing in parts of Hobbs for years. Just bag 'em up and give us a call, and we'll come and get 'em."

Given the time of year that Nate found the Hobbs campsite, we concluded that he was a victim of hypothermia. The journal provided some clues to his state of mind, which could have exacerbated the early symptoms of the condition. Most of his remains were found on a hillside near the water source at Bull Gap—less than three hundred yards from his campsite. We supposed that he wandered into the woods to get water and became disoriented; then he just laid himself down on the side of the hill and went to sleep.

Two years later, and still no one is looking for him.

In late May 2003, some two and one-half years after the Hobbs episode, a twenty-one-year-old policeman on a routine patrol saw what he mistook for a burglar scavenging a garbage bin behind a discount supermarket in Murphy,

North Carolina—and that was the end of the search for Eric Robert Rudolph. He was arrested and has been serving consecutive life terms since his sentencing.

The old hound never looked for, nor found, any more of Hobbs, but he did strike up a friendship during his walk to Bull Gap with a young sheriff's deputy, who adopted him that very day.

The author's wife, Margie Porter (far right), pals with her longtime friend Jenny (far left) and staffer Felicity (middle) at the annual Blaze of Glory party.

CHAPTER THIRTEEN
Cultures Collide

The group I've been calling, for lack of a better term, the hiking community is really a collection of groups. It's a subculture made up of a handful of smaller subcultures, and these don't always have much in common. Take, for example, what might be the two largest groups of hikers: retirees and college-age kids. The older group goes to the woods to enjoy some peace, calm, and fresh air as the reward for a life of hard work; the younger group, more hungry for "experience" than for relaxation, sees the Trail as a twenty-two-hundred-mile-long alternative-education class, with required courses in sex, drugs, philosophy, religion, guitar, and Hacky Sack. Throw in the rest of the bunch—the survivalists training for apocalypse, the midlife-crisis sufferers who left the family and sold the house, the few bona fide drifters (as opposed to the dimestore desperadoes who fake it)—and the resulting mix is like a big, squabbling family: they've got a name in common, but they sit at different tables when they all get together.

And as with a family, what causes hikers to forget their differences and band together, more than anything else, is the presence of outsiders.

Tonight is our Blaze of Glory party. More than a hundred people have shown up by foot and car for our annual event that celebrates both the thru-hiker season and the passing of my birthday.

Some of the staff have been challenged to a game of Texas hold 'em by a few of the local gentry of bankers, lawyers, developers, and real estate investors. The latter are cleaner, drive fancier cars, live in bigger houses, and smell a little prettier, and their drug of choice comes by prescription. The buy-in is one hundred dollars—big money compared with our normal ten-dollar play.

These people are part of my other universe, the business universe, in which I often feel artificial and uneasy. They don't fully understand me or the hiking community, and the sight of a businessman fraternizing with his customers on his birthday seems to both fascinate them and strike them as gross. They're acting like rich kids in a dive bar—slumming, and a little too pleased with themselves. And though they're intrigued by the adventure and spirit of the hikers—so, these are the people who choose to sleep on the ground—they judge, in the end, that the hiking life is some kind of a mistake. They think that we must be out here because we're defective in some way, and they're amusing themselves by looking for the defects.

But tonight is a special occasion. So they're playing cards and drinking with people they wouldn't trust to go near their children: men wearing long beards and women smelling like wet dogs—all with names such as Cornbread, Flounder, Flying Porkchop, Ramblin' Man, or Critter. The introductions go something like this: "Albert, meet Critter. Albert, Critter. Critter, Albert. Albert manages the bank. Critter once ate a roasted bat."

Margie is the one thing everyone can agree on: we all love her. Among the business leaders, she's known for her calm, plainspoken good sense and her charity involvement in the community; the hikers know her for her humor and hospitality; and everybody has heard about her cooking. With the help of friends, she has prepared a feast of barbecued baby back ribs, Southern coleslaw, squash casserole, grilled corn, tomato salad, and fresh sourdough bread. When the ribs run out, we have a hundred hamburgers and a hundred and fifty hot dogs.

The party has been officially in full swing since about nine o'clock, when Jenny, seeing me squeezing by in the breezeway carrying drinks above my head, hails me—"Look, Winnie!" Margie, beside her, starts laughing with a snort. I turn and see Jenny standing there with her elbows out and her two index fingers pointing in at her chest, grinning.

"Winnie, look! I got some new boobs!"

Jenny has been Margie's friend since grade school. She drove up from Atlanta for a weekend escape. She's an attractive woman, small and lively. Most of the time she's stretched out her full five-foot-three, because she's so often on her toes, bouncing around and flirting. Her short stature and puckish personality make her appear years younger than her age, and everything about her seems little—her nose, mouth, feet, hands. I met her within weeks of meeting Margie in college. That was more than eighteen years ago, and she still makes me laugh and smile today. Since my grandmother passed away thirteen years ago, she and Margie have been the only people in the world who can call me "Winnie," my childhood nickname, without getting a punch in the face.

I'm giving Jenny's new boobs a polite inspection with my eyes when, without warning, she yanks up her shirt, revealing a new, sporty bra with what looks like a pair of perky C's underneath. I take a gentleman's step back, spilling somebody's wine on the flagstones, and say, "I heard a rumor that you got a fresh set of sisters. Was that part of your divorce settlement?"

"No, I got them before he traded me in on a younger version. That's what I call getting while the getting's good."

"Can I touch them? See if you got your ex-husband's money's worth? Margie?"

"Of course you can," shouts Jenny. "Go ahead! Feel 'em! You can't tell the difference!"

I set down the wineglasses, no longer remembering anyway whom they were for, and reached out with both hands. "I'll believe that when I—wow! Firm, soft, a little bigger than the old ones. How can we get some of these, Margie?"

Margie intervenes—slaps my hand, smiles, and says, "Settle. That's enough, Winnie."

Jenny laughs and gives me a hug—the third since she got in, and the most wobbly so far. "Thanks for inviting me. Now. Where are the singles?"

"Margie, I will leave that up to you, but keep her away from Trudge."

"Who is Trudge, Margie?" Jenny asks.

"He's an afterthought," Margie says. "Keep your distance."

The hikers circle the keg of Pabst Blue Ribbon and drink standing up; the white-collar types drink red wine and vodka and do their best to strike lounging poses. A banker sits in a stained canvas director's chair, shifting his weight every three seconds and slapping at bugs; a real estate agent leans against a wall with her ankles crossed. Different styles of drinking, but with the same destination. By ten o'clock the groups are mixing freely. Trish likes the new spirit of equality. She has planted herself, like a Venus flytrap, in the breezeway, between the poker table and the bar, and she's trying to take a bite out of every tall man going by—white collar, blue collar, or no collar.

Trish is in her midforties, divorced, a honey blond who takes as much pride in the curves of her body as in the clothes she covers them with. A slim, full-breasted woman, she can turn heads when she enters a room, and likes doing it. She imagines that she enjoys intellectual conversation, but is unable to hold her attention long enough to engage in the discourse; what she really enjoys is splitting hairs over luxury brand names, making known her preferences for Mercedes over Volvo and Louis Vuitton over Coach. She also likes to think of herself as a kindly, concerned friend to the local married men, a listener and a comforter. But the concern and comfort she offers tend to go beyond friendship.

I meet Trish's height requirement, so my turn with her "friendship" comes when I venture out to refill Jenny's wineglass and Trish, meeting me on the way, staggers into me and pins me to the wall. She pulls close enough to my face that I can smell the red wine on her breath and see the purple tinge to her teeth and the loose rolling of her eyes. Her lipstick has been recently reapplied, and not well. I tell her she looks lovely tonight.

"Yes. Thank you. Winton. How are you doing? You look well. Are you still running? Margie lost some weight! What do you think about that? She looks—real goooood."

"Yes, I am still running, and Margie always looks great to me. But now you mention it, the sex has been a lot better, lately, Trish. In fact, I don't think I've ever been—"

"Fantastic. Now tell me really. What about you? How are you really doing?"

I look for an escape, but she moves in closer, slumping against me heavily. "I am really doing okay, but could use a drink. How about you?"

"That would be lovely," she says. "Red if you got it, and you if you don't." Here she tries a flirty light touch on the nose, but misses, and briefly hooks one of my nostrils with a fake nail.

"I've got plenty of red, Trish," I say. "Believe me."

Trish backs away from the wall and turns her attention toward the view from the balcony. I fill drinks and walk back to the safety of my wife, who has been secretly watching the entire exchange from the poker table with Jenny and Nancy. Margie is smiling at me and laughing. I'd really rather have a grilled cheese sandwich than sleep with another woman.

"Marjorie, you are no help at all!" I tell her.

"It was funny! And you looked completely in control of the situation." She grins, dealing a hand.

Alpine peeks at his cards and has what looks like an allergic reaction, fidgeting in the chair, his shoulders shifting left and then right, as if he's trying to scratch an itch on his back. Felicity, at Margie's left, sits straight up, her eyes cold and her face and posture rigid, motionless—except for her right pinky finger, which is tapping out a dead giveaway on the green felt table. Margie leans back, sipping her wine while her signature smile plays at the corners of her mouth.

Rolling away from the table in her office chair, she folds and gets out cheap, winking at the bluffers.

"What did Trish want, anyway?" Margie asks.

"Me. Unless you give me that glass of Hellbender in your hands."

I take the nearly full glass of that Crane Creek red wine from Margie, use my shirt to remove the lipstick from the edges, and give her a kiss on the cheek. I tell her to send rescue if I'm not back in three minutes.

Billy's ready to play, but no one is sure if he knows how. His thick, white beard, along with his dark, Serpico-style sunglasses, hide all expression. He looks left and then right and finally back toward the mound of chips in the center of the table, and shouts, "Hold 'em or fold 'em—because I'm all in!" He shoves his meager pile of chips forward.

"But it's my bet, Billy," Felicity says.

"Fold," Alpine moans.

Back at the balcony, I find Trish working on her latest victim. "I see that you've met Trudge," I say, handing her Margie's used wine.

"Trudge. Izzat your trail name?" Trish asks.

"I sure hope it isn't my real name!" Trudge says. Trish slaps him on the shoulder, and they lean against one another, laughing drunkenly.

"I'll leave you kids to it," I say, lurching off.

For about two years now—long enough to have developed a far-traveling reputation as a ladies' man—Trudge has been traversing the Trail, doing more driving than hiking, but mostly just hanging out wherever the crowds seemed to be headed. In his midthirties, an attractive, tall, fit man, with an engaging smile and a Southern gentility, he's generally more well kept than most hikers, favoring short hair, a clean shave, and pressed shirts. The story Trudge told me was that he used to own a brewery in Virginia, but sold it a few years ago, along with everything else he owned, after his wife and kids were killed in a car accident by a drunk driver. The event rattled his world so badly that he decided to shed his old life and go out and hike the Appalachian Trail.

He has never caused trouble, but we've always kept him at arm's length. The reason we can't trust him is that his story is just too familiar. How I Was Exiled from the World: every twentieth hiker through the store plays a new variation on the tale. The business went bust, the fast life got dull, the wealth and success failed to satisfy, the wife and kids died. The version of the story depends on who is telling it. We don't exactly disbelieve it, but we can't believe it either. On the Trail, the stories people tell about themselves are mostly a way of saving time.

What could be said for Trudge was that he followed a consistent script with regard to the main points: always a wife, always a car accident, always a drunk driver, and always the Appalachian Trail. But the number of kids and the type of company he sold seemed to change, as did the source of his mysterious income. Secondhand versions of Trudge's story featured trust funds, life-insurance policies, stocks, bonds, patents, royalties, and more.

We would find out later that there were warrants for Trudge's arrest in four states and that the Secret Service had gotten involved in the search. He befriended women and took liberties with their bank accounts. He was caught somewhere in Virginia.

I'm back at the poker table, taking in the action, when Nancy, having gone off for some food, comes back down the gravel pathway toward us with hurried steps. She has a big-eyed expression of flustered disgust on her face.

Margie sees her first. "Nancy, what's wrong?"

"You wouldn't believe what just happened to me!"

"Try me," I say.

"Well, I was—hold on. I think I have a rock in my shoe."

Alpine studies an alpine lake, on the A.T. somewhere north of Georgia.

Nancy, another friend of Margie's, came to Blairsville by way of Boca Raton, Florida, where she acquired the habit of overdressing. The gravel, the bugs, the grill smoke, and the close brushes with filthy hikers have kept her outfit in constant danger since she arrived, and she has spent much of the evening smoothing, straightening, grooming, and recomposing her attire. She steadies herself on Margie's shoulder, pulls off her right silver Mary Jane shoe and shakes it a few times, drops it to the ground, and slides her foot back in, hopping on the gravel. She adjusts the diamond pendant on her neck with one hand and drags the other through her short blond hair as if she is trying to wash something out. Nancy is a fast talker who will swerve in and out of her thoughts. I have to concentrate a little harder when she talks so that I don't get lost.

"Do you smell that? Oh, Margie, I like your outfit, where did you get it? I have some shoes that would look—"

"Nancy, focus! What happened?" Margie demands.

"Oh, yeah. There's this smelly hiker guy over there next to the trash can. With a pack—he must've just come off the Trail. I went over to throw away this half-empty bottle of diet soda that I had in my car. After I dumped it into the garbage, the hiker guy with the pack walks over, starts digging into the trash can. He must've had half his body in the damn thing. After a couple of seconds, he pulls out my diet soda and drinks it! And then he reaches back into the garbage can and pulls out a half-eaten piece of pizza. I never have seen anything like that before. Who are these people?"

Margie looks over at me with a smile. "Pirate's back."

Dennis Selburg, trail name Pirate, is a retired Navy SEAL. He grew up in an orphanage outside Pensacola, Florida. He joined the Navy at seventeen and was sent to Vietnam. In the late seventies and early eighties, he chased drug runners throughout the Atlantic, the Caribbean, and the Gulf of Mexico. Pirate's last major operation was as a participant in the invasion of Panama in 1989. The event became known as Operation Nifty Package, part of the larger surprise attack ordered by President George H. W. Bush to extract dictator Manuel Noriega from Panama and bring him to the United States for trial on drug-trafficking charges. Noriega managed to flee the invasion, but was discovered a few days later hiding in the Holy See's embassy in Panama. The U.S. military bombarded the embassy with loud music in a game of psychological warfare. Noriega surrendered a few days later. I once asked Pirate what he did during the invasion, and he said, "I was in charge of music."

After his retirement, he decided to hike the A.T. That was many years ago, and he is still out there walking. I doubt that any razor or scissors has touched a hair on his head in all that time. People who see him on the Trail often take him for a full-time vagabond, but he's not homeless; he has properties in

Florida—a house in Fort Walton Beach and several acres in Melrose, and he stops in to visit them every few years.

Now in his late fifties, he's still as strong and as bold as the music he blasted at Noriega, and his beard, even on a trail full of beards, is one of the most famous of all. I have often wondered whether the beard is for appearance or for food storage. It's black with dashes of white creeping in on the edges, and its frizzes point in every direction, giving him a freshly electrocuted look. What can be seen of the skin on his face is notched with the deep, leathery wrinkles of a hard-fought life. The hair on his head matches his beard, and he keeps it most often pulled back into a ponytail and covered with a hat or bandanna. We ask him what came first—the name Pirate or the piratical getup—but he won't say.

Pirate has lived on and off at the store for several years. His days of hiking are starting to slow. At first he spent a few weeks here, then maybe a month, and now it's between four and six months of the year before he heads off to another location or adventure. He has become a part of our family, as well as the hostel's unofficial chef.

I never assigned him any specific task; he would find things to do on his own, and work from sunup to sundown. Nearly every morning he would be up before five preparing breakfast for the hikers—pancakes mostly, but if he liked the group it was eggs, biscuits, bacon, and sausage. At night, it was sloppy joes, spaghetti and meatballs, Spam casserole, or his favorite fourteen-bean chili with homemade cornbread. He would empty the trash, clean bathrooms, fix what needed fixing; one day he might be a plumber and a cook, the next an electrician and a mechanic. And at night he would kick back and play entertainment director; he liked hosting trivia contests.

He loved all the holidays and birthdays, but Halloween was his favorite. Last year, he spent three days turning the hostel into a haunted house. He had secretly collected stuff from thrift stores and garage sales for months, and what he couldn't find he bought at a Walmart in Murphy. Sierra loved it and invited all her friends from school to share in the magic. Many left crying with pee stains in their pants.

Pirate bought all the food for the hikers. It was his way of giving back. Pirate never asked for money and often refused it when it was offered. The staff had to make him a tip jar and remind people that their hostel fees weren't buying the hot meals. Some hikers still complained that the eggs were too runny, the biscuits too hard, or the cornbread too dry. However, most tried to throw a few dollars into the pot, and each year one or two people would send a check for fifty or a hundred dollars, made out to Pirate's Magic Fund.

This is one of my favorite Pirate stories: once, on the balcony, Pirate was sitting on a rock next to the building. He was wearing a pair of silver-wire-rimmed sunglasses and enjoying the day's sun and the procession of people while drinking a cup of coffee from a big titanium mug. He was wearing his standard hiking clothes: dirty shorts with holes in the pockets and a black shirt with a blue blaze, reading "Hiker Trash." His beard was filled with white crumbs from his morning biscuit. A clean-shaven Harley rider dressed in three thousand dollars' worth of leather—thinking perhaps that he was looking at an ex–Hell's Angel down on his luck—reached into his pocket as he left the store and threw a handful of change into Pirate's fresh cup of coffee. Pirate turned to the motorcyclist, shifted his sunglasses down on his nose, smiled, and watched the man descend the stairs to the parking lot. He didn't say a word. He reached into his coffee, dug out the coins, took another sip, and went back to watching the crowd. Thirty years in the Navy, a few good real estate investments, and a regiment of loyal friends have provided him with all that he needs.

Nancy pulls a bottle of perfume from her purse, sprays her hands, then rubs a little underneath her nose. "I can't get away from that hiker smell. I think it has singed the hair of my nose."

I tell her it'll grow on her in a couple of hours.

"Yeah, I bet it'll grow on me. Like a fungus."

"Nancy," Margie breaks in, "let's go get you a drink and a bottle of Purell. Winton, you go help Pirate get settled in and point him to the shower. I think I can smell him on the breeze myself."

I find Pirate standing next to his pack at the base of the stairs talking with Alpine. "Pirate, welcome back. You certainly freaked out one of the locals, with the garbage can trick again. Nice job."

"I was thirsty."

"Staff fixed up a new room for you downstairs. Want to see it?"

"Why not? But, first, I brought you a little gift." He reaches down into his pack, pulls out a brown paper bag, and hands it to me.

I pull out a half-empty Mason jar. "Corn liquor. Thanks. What happened to the other half of it?"

"I get thirsty a lot."

Alpine and I lead Pirate down into the hostel to show him his room, but find a sea of people crowded inside, blocking our way through. I step back outside.

"Pirate, I don't think you've had a shower in—what? About two weeks?"

"Three. At least three."

"Good. I'll let you lead."

Pirate enters the room, pauses in the doorway, raises his hiking stick a few inches above his head, and starts walking. Alpine and I go behind him, and his stink goes in front. The sea of people parts. Moses would be proud.

I unlock the door that leads to the stairwell. We open another small door under the stairs and usher Pirate in. He has to duck his head to get through the door. The space is about four feet wide and about ten feet deep. A single light floats overhead; bookshelves cover one side, and on the other is a single bed pushed tight against the wall. On the wall at the end is a painting of an old sailboat hanging at a three-inch tilt. Pirate doesn't get excited about much, and with all the beard and hair it's hard to tell whether he's excited or not. All his expression is in his eyes, and that's how we know he likes it.

"We call it Pirate's House. Home sweet home!" says Alpine.

"It's perfect. Reminds me of ship life."

When Alpine and Jennifer finally meet, most of the crowd has moved out of the hostel and is outside trying to regain some fresh air. We have climbed to the top of the stairs of the hostel and are moving down the gravel pathway toward the parking lot when Jennifer pulls into a spot just inches away from where we started our turn up the stairs toward the shop. She honks the horn to alert us of her arrival.

"Well, Alpine. There she is."

"Who?"

"Jennifer. The one you keep hearing about. And it looks like the boyfriend is still in tow."

"That's all right with me. I told you, I have enough on my plate. You think I—"

Then Jennifer steps out of the driver-side door, and Alpine stops talking.

John rolls out of the passenger side and rises shakily to his full height. He leans back into the car, pulls out a bottle, and comes over, shoving the end of the bottle at me before he makes it to hello. "Broughtcha summathishere Johnny Walker fertha party," he drawls. "Izz great stuff; want some?"

I tell him thanks, but no thanks. He goes stumbling up the stairs toward the crowd on the balcony before he can be introduced to Alpine.

Jennifer runs up and greets me with a hug. "Win-tone!" she sings out. "Sorry we're late."

"You're not late. We are just getting started. Jennifer, have you met Alpine? He worked with us last year."

"No. Maybe. You look familiar. Oh, yeah. You helped me with my pack last year; I remember. You're the Army guy?"

"Yes. Nice to officially meet you, Jennifer. I've heard a lot about you."

And Jennifer says with a smile: "What have you heard?"

For the rest of the night, I see the two of them separate only once, and that is when Jennifer is trying to find John, who passed out on one of the stone picnic tables in the back of the building about an hour after he arrived.

On toward morning, a crowd of people, swaying with drink, gathers around the poker table to watch the final two players battle it out. Four cards lie on the table—K♣, Q♦, 8♠, and 5♥—beside a pot of several hundred dollars.

Tony, Nancy's husband, holds a slight lead in the chip count. Across from him, Billy Bumblefoot sits motionless and unreadable behind his big, dark Serpico frames, waiting for his opponent's next move. Tony stacks and restacks his chips with one hand and takes a lemon drop shooter to his mouth with the other. He leans back in his chair and wipes the sugar from his finger onto the upper left sleeve of his Tommy Bahama shirt. On the top of his shiny head, beads of sweat are forming. He looks to each side as if seeking help from a face in the crowd.

"Hey, Jimmy Buffett," Billy croaks sleepily. "Your move. I said that I'm all in; do you need me to count it?"

"Maybe so. You've been all in about fourteen times tonight. Who knows how much it is this time? Every time I turn around you're going all in."

"Then I'm either the dumbest son of a bitch in the woods, or I know something you don't know."

"You've got nothing. You've had nothing all night, Bumblefoot. I'm all in. Show me your cards, hiker boy."

"You first!"

Tony flips over his cards, revealing K♦ and Q♥, and stands up to pace, stretch, puff his cheeks, rub his hands. Billy impassively shows a pair of twos and sits as still as before.

The dealer calls out "Last card!" and throws the top card to the side and slowly rolls over the last card—the two of hearts. Hikers cheer all around— the young ones, the old ones, the washed and unwashed. Tonight we're one team, and Billy's win is our win. Tony's knees buckle, and he leans against his chair. He grabs the empty lemon-shooter glass and tries to suck out one last drop from the bottom. Finally, Billy removes his sunglasses, slides his chair back, stands, and extends a gracious hand to Tony.

"I was right," Tony says. "You had nothing."

"But I got something when I needed it," Billy says. "What's for breakfast, Pirate?"

And sweeping the chips into an old Tilley hat, Billy hands over a sizable donation to Pirate's Magic Fund.

Some interpret this anonymous rock art as "love." Others say it's "live." But most agree that the trail is about both: loving life and living it—with heart.

CHAPTER FOURTEEN
The Lady's Slipper Killer

"Excuse me, sir—sir? Sir, excuse me. I was wondering if you could answer a question for me about this flower." Billy and I are passing time on the porch when the woman strolls up, blossom in hand.

I'd guess she's in her early forties, and I can't help but notice her perky breasts beneath a form-fitting top. Her cheeks, lips, and forehead also look to be fresh from a little touch-up, compliments of the plastic surgeon. The skin seems a little too firm and a little too smooth, stretched over her bones like the plastic packaging of cheap cheese. Her attire, complete with a multipocket jungle vest from some glossy catalog, is outdoor wear only in the sense that it looks good on models posed next to trees. Hiding behind Mom are two boys, about five and seven, waiting for the answer about the treasure they have found. The woman hands me the torn carcass of one of the rarest and most exquisite creatures in these woods, and Billy and I can't miss the contrast between the flower's natural beauty and her storebought version.

Billy, next to me, sees the dead thing and sucks a gasp of shock through his teeth.

"It's a pink lady's slipper," I tell her. "Some, like me, call it a moccasin flower."

Cypripedium acaule is a terrestrial orchid that grows in these mountains that surround my house. The plant has two wide basal leaves and a single green stalk growing to about a foot high. In late spring it bears a pink flower that looks like a slipper. Transplanting the moccasin from the wild is strongly discouraged because the chance of survival is almost nil; besides which, harvesting the plant in a national forest is illegal, and she got this one from the side of our highway that is clearly part of the Chattahoochee National Forest. The woman turns and kneels down next to the children and shows them the corpse, already growing pale and slack, and gets it almost right, in her childlike voice: "Well, boys—there you have it! It's called a pink moccasin slipper! Isn't it pretty?"

I tell her it was prettier before she killed it.

After the woman and her sons leave, Alpine comes bouncing up the stairs and runs over to where Billy and I are standing. There is nervous excitement in his voice, and he seems to be having trouble gathering his thoughts. We're not even sure at first whether he's talking to us or to himself.

"I don't know what it is about this place," he says. "There's something special, I don't know what. Every time I come here, it's like—it's like all the burdens of the world have been lifted off my shoulders. It's spiritual. I tell you, it's spiritual, man. Thanks for letting me come back, Winton. I really know this is the place where I am supposed to be."

"What have you been smoking? Damn, I told you not to do that stuff when you're working."

"The man's talking about *looooooove.*" Billy sings the last word in a swooping falsetto.

"That's right," Alpine says. He looks about as serious as I've ever seen him. "Jennifer. She's the one. I know it, I just know it."

I remind him that he's known her only three days.

"Three and a half," he says. "She likes to do nearly everything I like to do: hike, climb, mountain bike, surf. We're already talking about doing a southbound thru-hike this year."

"What about John?"

Alpine is quiet for a moment. He bends down and gives Sky a rub behind the ears. "Well. She's been looking to get away from him for a while. She's trying to figure out how to tell him. Things between them have been pretty rough."

"And what about you not wanting to get involved in a relationship right now. Remember? Sit back and enjoy life?"

"This is different. Come on, dude. Give me a break."

"Yeah, dude," Billy says, chucking me in the shoulder. "Give the boy a break; the ink on those divorce papers has had plenty of time to dry by now. We're talking about love here. This is about nature. Springtime. We're animals, you know. This is about chemical reactions, pheromones—Sergeant, are you blushing?"

"Thanks, Billy. I knew you would understand," Alpine says, shoving his hands into his pockets. "But actually we're taking things slow. I really like this girl. We have our first official, uh, date, tomorrow night."

"There you are, Winton," Billy says. "An officer and a gentleman. Better bring some flowers, Sergeant."

I tell him I know where he can find a lady's slipper corsage.

Back in the store, Felicity helps a hiker with boots, Nate shuffles backpacks around on the wall, and Buddy cheerfully hollers into the phone.

"It a timberback rattlesnake, you idiot."

"Take a long stick and push him off the trail," he says. There's a pause.

"Well, try a longer stick. This ain't rocket—" Pause. "Well, how high do you think you can jump?" Pause. "You want me to what? Send somebody up to get you."

Buddy covers the receiver with his hand and looks over at me.

"Eh, Winton. I got some kid on the mountain. He says a snake is blocking the Trail, and he wants one of us to go up and help 'im out of there. What do you want me to do?"

"Where's he at?"

"Where you at?" Pause. "He hears cars on the road, and he's next to a big Forest Service sign."

He's across the street, about two hundred yards away on the Trail.

"I'll go up there and get him."

"We're on our way." Buddy says, and hangs up the phone.

"Why did you hang up on him?"

"What? Did you need to talk to the snake?"

Snakes, as such, don't bother me; what bothers me is the talent they have for unpleasant surprises. Snakes stay out of sight. In the time it takes me to reach this kid, this rattler might have time to hide itself and get angry—and then we'll be no better off than before. As a rule, I simply avoid snakes as much as I can. Luckily for me, there are those who admire snakes and will go looking for them.

"Hey, Billy! You want to go catch a snake?"

Billy is seated on the top step outside the store with Sky by his side. They both get up at once. The dog's tail starts wagging; if Billy had a tail, it would be wagging too.

"What kind?"

"Sounds like a timberback rattler."

"Where is it?"

"Holding some kid hostage on the Trail about a hundred yards up."

"What?"

"Just follow me."

Billy follows at my heels, and Sky at his. Within a few moments we see the scared hostage: a heavyset, teenaged boy wearing baggy jeans and a Bob Marley T-shirt that hangs just above his knees. His lower lip, which is trembling with fear, is pierced with a gold ring.

I call out to the boy and ask his name.

"My name is Chris. Thanks for coming."

The snake, still coiled in the middle of the trail, has turned back to face Billy and me. I step aside and let eager Billy come around to within a few feet of it. Sky, keeping her eyes on the snake, makes a wide half-circle down and then back up the steep embankment, comes around next to Chris, and sits at his feet. Billy starts talking to the snake in a low, slow tone. He gives her some compliments about her size—she's about five feet—and tells her it's time to move on. When he decides to talk to me, he does so out of the side of his mouth, as though he doesn't want the snake to hear what he says.

"Hey, Winton. You think you could get Sky to speak?"

"What do you want her to say?"

"Make her bark, smartass!"

"Sky, speak!" I yell.

Sky lifts her head, perks her ears, and waits for a confirmation of the command.

"Sky, speak! Speak, girl!

She stands up, barks three times. The snake turns and challenges Sky, causing the hair on her back to rise; she crouches and inches cautiously forward, growling, then giving three more barks. The distraction gives Billy time to move within arm's reach of the five-foot monster, and with the speed of lightning he snatches the snake behind the head. Then he turns toward me, putting the face and fangs of the beast within inches of my head. I jump back and catch my heel on a root, and that sends me tumbling down fifteen feet of embankment and into a thicket of briars and poison ivy.

Billy screams out happily, "Look at her! Isn't she incredible! Damn, what a rush! Are you okay down there? I was just trying to show you the snake! Why'd you jump?"

I shout a few curses at him while he carries the snake off into the woods. Then, under the anxious supervision of Sky, who trots back and forth, nosing my arms and legs, I disentangle myself from the briars and climb back up the embankment. Chris holds out his hand when I get within a few feet of the trail. He's not strong enough to help me much—I'm a big man—but I appreciate the gesture and take his hand.

"Sir, thank you," he says. "I really didn't know what else to do. I really didn't want to hurt it. Your friend there isn't going to kill it, is he?"

"Billy? Oh, no. Billy prefers copperheads. He says the timberback rattlers taste like tree bark. Where you headed after this?"

"Well, I was going to hike for a few months. . . ."

Sky goes off into the woods to check on Billy and the snake. As we wait for their return, Chris fills me in on his parents' bitter divorce and how his family just doesn't understand him anymore. He and his girlfriend broke up, and he needed to "get far away from all that noise in my head. Life just isn't worth all this hassle," he says. His father is a financial consultant with Lehman Brothers and travels most of the time. His mother is a commercial real estate agent in Atlanta. When he was younger, his dad took him camping on top of Blood Mountain; this is one of the few enjoyable memories of his father that he possesses. He left his house a little more than a week ago without telling anybody where he was going. He has been camping out in the woods under a large rock overhang on the Freeman trail, which skirts Blood Mountain and connects to the A.T. on each end.

Our encounter is on the A.T. only a couple hundred yards from the store. But I don't tell him that we knew he was there. We had gotten word about the campsite a few days earlier; we just hadn't seen the camper.

"It's unlikely that anyone is looking for me. My mom was in New York, and my dad, well, I don't know where he is this week."

Cimarron sizes up a hike.

After a few minutes, Billy returns with Sky, and we all sit together on the trail while Chris talks. Having a human audience for the first time in many days seems to change him for the better; after a while his conversation turns from his complaints, his fears, and his pains to his fondest childhood memories, his proudest moments, and then to things he wants to do and see. Some things are worth the hassle after all. He talks about walking the Appalachian Trail, spending a summer in Yosemite, and traveling to Peru to see Incan ruins. He doesn't know why he is talking to us, and we don't know either. I want to say something, feel compelled to offer some kind of fatherly advice, but the voices in the wind keep telling me to shut up. The same voices may be whispering to Billy, who stretches himself out on the ground and chews a piece of grass while he takes in Chris's story.

Finally, Chris stands up, shoulders his pack, and picks up his Adidas duffle bag. He kicks a small rock off the trail, and starts walking.

"Where you going from here?" I ask him.

"Home," he says. "Right now I want to go home. Thank you."

I sit on the trail a few more minutes and watch Chris until his pack fades around the bend. In a few minutes he will be down at the shop.

As Billy and I head back there ourselves, I remember I want to ask him something. "Billy, did you hear that last thing Alpine said, about John, before he took off this morning?"

"What thing? The thing about 'lockdown?' "

"Yeah, lockdown. That's it. Making sure you heard what I heard."

Alpine had asked off early, in consideration of his date with Jennifer; he needed to clean out his car and get a haircut. When I told him he could go, he had thanked me, and then: "Oh, I almost forgot. You may want to watch your back; I'm not sure how old John's going to take the news. She's supposed to tell him tonight. Apparently, he can be kind of a loose cannon, so I wouldn't answer your door until you know for certain who's on the other side. We call it 'lockdown' in the Army. Thanks again; see you later."

With that, Alpine had skipped away like a little kid on his way to the patch to pick blueberries for the first time.

I tell Billy I don't understand why John would be coming after me. "Why would the guy blame me for what happened that night? If he wanted to keep his girlfriend from trading him in at that party, he shouldn't have taken a nap on the picnic table."

"Loose cannon, like Alpine said. And the guy ain't the brightest crayon in the box."

I pluck at some grass by the trailside, and we walk along quietly until I put a nagging thought into words: "Billy—you think that kid came out here to kill himself?"

"I don't know," Billy says. "If he did, it looks to me like he postponed it."

This isn't the first time that I've had the strange feeling that we have intervened or helped someone take a different path (literally, sometimes) or make another choice—and it will not be the last. The store is a crossroads, and, living here, I get to watch people choose their ways, make their turns—left or right, farther or back. For many, these mountains offer refreshment from the everyday, a place to quiet the mind and revitalize the senses; but some come here to seek a more permanent escape. I meet a few every year who tell me that they went into the woods feeling that they'd reached the rope's end, and—for those who talk about such things—hiking usually does them good. Nature silences a troubled mind because it is so envelopingly slow. Our agitations of mind don't touch it; our worries pass through it, bounce off it, but can't disturb it, and eventually they just go away, as though from sheer embarrassment. Without our usual means of winding ourselves into anxiety—the house, the car, the bills, the diet—we simply must find other thoughts, and I think that is why hikers on this Trail speak so often of discovering things they had forgotten and of being reminded of how precious life can be. Once the encounter with nature has cleared the static from your head, what remains is what you knew all along, the values that sustain you. In the case of the young hiker Chris, I don't believe that he had the happiest family, but he did have a family that he decided he couldn't abandon.

"What do you think it was that made him alter course, Billy—if, in fact, our theory is right? The pine air? The birdsong? The breathtaking view from Blood Mountain?"

"I think it was the snake," Billy says.

He grins and chews his grass awhile. Then he remembers a question of his own.

"Hey, Winton," he says. "That woman with the moccasin flower—whereabout do you suppose she is now?"

"I'd say right about now she's doing what Chris is doing," I say. "Turning around."

There's an ending to that story about the lady's slipper—and its executioner.

When I told the woman and her sons that the flower was prettier before they killed it, the two boys, both horrified and fascinated to hear the word killed, drew closer to their mother but let their eyes widen and their mouths fall open. They sensed my anger better than she did.

That was only the third moccasin flower I'd ever seen. The first two were alive, and I remember they had, in the highest degree, that special kind of beauty that only things in nature can have: the kind of beauty that doesn't care whether anyone sees it. The flowers were content just to be perfect and rooted to the earth, unwatched and alone on a mountainside. Nature isn't made for us. Wild things are beautiful because they don't belong to us.

The moccasin-flower woman said she had one more question, while Billy and I were handy there on the balcony. "At your service," Billy said to her, bowing low as he shot me a glance.

"Ooh, a gentleman!" she said with a giggle. "Anyway, my question is—the map I was reading said this was a wildlife management area. Well, I want to know: where are all the animals?"

Sometimes the stars align themselves to reveal the ignorance of humanity—leaving me to wonder, in the face of questions like the one I've just been asked, how our species managed to survive all these centuries. Maybe it's simply a matter of time until we slip on the final banana peel, or maybe there truly is a forgiving God. But the history of our dealings with the natural world may prove that if we destroy ourselves, we'll do it by mistake and probably without even noticing.

"You know, that's a good question," I said. "Where are all the animals, Billy?"

"You're in luck, miss! They were on loan to the Atlanta Zoo for a while, and now they're back," Billy said. "If you'd come last week, you would've missed 'em."

"Billy used to be a keeper at the wildlife management area," I explained.

Billy pulled out his journal and pen from his back pocket and proceeded to write down the feeding times for bear, rabbit, skunk, raccoon, deer, turkey, and red-tailed hawk, and told the lady that the best place to view these events was down at Helton Creek near the top of the waterfalls.

"Just go up the highway about a mile and a half and turn right when you see the sign for Helton Creek Cottages," Billy said. "Then just go as straight as you can. You'll see the big tent. You can't miss it. But you better leave quickly or you will miss the bear feeding. That's one of my favorites."

The boys tugged on their mother's jungle vest, begging to leave. She thanked Billy for the information, and the three ran off together to a white Cadillac Escalade. Which, around the time Alpine came up to tell us of his new love, would just have started its bumpy ride over fifteen or twenty miles of the nastiest dirt road in the state, on its way to a petting zoo that didn't exist.

The lady's slipper got her revenge.

Heading south to Florida, a yellow-blazer (road-walker) gives a backward salute to Mountain Crossings, a few yards behind him on the Union County side of U.S. 19/129.

CHAPTER FIFTEEN
Just Left of Crazy

Morning, 4:56. Margie was curled up in the bed with Sierra and Allison. I had been pushed to the couch in the middle of the night and couldn't get back to sleep. Sky was in a swirl against my legs at the end of the couch. A cool breeze found a crack in the seal of the south window and nudged its way across my face. I yanked the blanket over my head and forced my eyes to close. Sky mimicked my movement, and I felt her coil herself a little tighter. A second small breeze came from the opposite direction and seeped through the blanket and down the back of my neck. Sky lifted her head off my leg and let out a low growl followed by a whimper. I heard a light tapping sound against the stone, coming from the breezeway. I threw off my blanket. Sky jumped down and followed me to the door. The tapping got a little louder. I looked through the peephole of the old door, and instantly the sound stopped. Under the dim light, I saw a shadow float northbound across the back wall of the breezeway.

"What are you talking about?" I asked the dog. "Just a hiker getting an early start. Come on, girl. Let's get back to sleep."

Sky let out another low growl and retreated underneath the coffee table. I told her she was crazy and crossed the den to turn up the electric heaters.

That's when the room started to shake—the whole room, and the whole house: dishes rattling in the kitchen, the hardwood floors rocking like a boat on the ocean. My brain couldn't find a reference point for what was happening, nor could I command my feet, my arms, or my mouth to move.

The shaking lasted maybe ten seconds and stopped; and then the quiet of the morning sounded quieter than it ever had before.

Margie jumped out of bed and stepped into the den. "What the hell was that? It felt like the building was crashing down," she said as she nervously ran her hand through her tangled hair.

I told her I thought it was an earthquake.

"No. Is that what you think it was?"

"I guess. I've never been in one, but if I ever were, I think that's what it would feel like."

"Winton, Georgia doesn't have earthquakes."

"I know Georgia doesn't have earthquakes. That's why I don't know why we just had an earthquake."

"What else could it have been?"

"What else makes a whole house move?"

At this, Margie seemed to change her mind.

"You get the kids, take 'em outside," I said. "And I'll check on the folks in the hostel."

I stepped outside into the breezeway with Sky and descended the stairs. Pirate was already ushering everyone out of the hostel and away from the building. "Wake up, everybody! Time to get a move on!" Hikers were stumbling out of the door, rubbing eyes, shaking heads, trying to regain their sense of balance. Pirate looked as if he knew what to do in an earthquake. That made one of us.

"How long you been up, Pirate?"

Pirate considered this question while caressing his beard. Never one to waste words, he decided that one was enough for an answer. "Hour," he said.

"What's for breakfast?"

"Pancakes. Sausage. Bagels. Pop-Tarts."

"What do you think? Earthquake?"

He nodded, just once. "Four-point-eight, four-point-nine. I've been in bigger."

"Think another will come behind it? Aftershocks?"

"Doubt it. Or at least not one that we'll notice."

"How many more in the hostel?"

"Think this is all of them, except for the two kids who came in last night sometime."

This caught the attention of a woman standing nearby. "Their names are Brandon and Braden," she said. "Oh, and my name is Molly. I mean Groovy. I'm still getting used to my new trail name. You must be Mr. Porter."

Groovy looked to be in her early sixties. She wore her hair down, without clips, pins, or bands; it had the rich gray color of ash and a consistency between wheat and wire, and it drifted just above her shoulders. She had a plastic sunflower tucked above her left ear—either it was always there, or she had found the time, even in the middle of an earthquake, to put it back in place—and she was wearing an oversized nightshirt that hung below her knees. Screen-printed in the center of the shirt was what appeared to be a picture of her grandchildren. I was forced to look at her lips when she spoke because her voice was soft and quiet. I thought that she did this on purpose.

"Are you the mother?" I asked her.

"Oh, no. I met them on the Trail a few days ago. They're twins. Nice boys. They say they're nineteen, but I can't believe that. I think they're fifteen or sixteen. They sleep a lot. You want me to wake them up?" With her breathy voice and the faraway hint of a smile on her face, her air of distracted amusement, she looked as though she were trying to remember the punch line of a joke someone had told her a long time ago. The ex-flower-child mystique must have explained her trail name. Her hands made slow, curving motions in the air when she spoke.

"No, let them sleep," I said. "Pirate, I'll leave you in charge here. I'm going back to check on the girls and the shop."

In the breezeway, Margie was still standing on wobbly knees with a bug-eyed look on her face. Allison and Sierra, beside her, looked happy and excited. Margie said with motherly concern, "Do you think we should take the girls down the mountain? What should we do?"

"It's fine, just a tremor. Right, Pirate?"

Pirate nodded.

"What does Pirate know about earthquakes?"

"Margie, he's been in earthquakes before. He said it'll take a lot more than that to bring this old building down. Tell her, Pirate."

Pirate raised his hands, palms up.

Margie, rolling her eyes, turned and led the girls back into the house. It was too cold to be standing outside in our pajamas, talking about earthquakes. "You think you're funny," she said. "I think you're crazy."

Sierra marched to the center of the living room and chimed in next, trying to imitate her mother's eye-roll, folding her little arms across her chest. "I know you're crazy, Daddy."

Followed by Allison: "I don't think you're crazy, Daddy."

"Thank you, Allison!"

"Well, maybe just a little." Allison laughed, let my hand go, and joined the girls' team. She was developing quite a sense of humor.

"I am so outnumbered in this house," I said. "I'll show you crazy, girls. Daddy's going to run up Blood Mountain this morning in under thirty-five minutes. Now, that's what I call crazy!"

I hefted Allison and tickled her, making faces to let her know I was serious about being crazy. "I want to come, Daddy!" she squealed, her hands in my hair.

"Daddy's got to go it alone this time. Sorry, girl." I set her down and knelt beside her, keeping her in a hug.

"What if we have another earthquake while you're running?" Margie said with a cautious smile.

"I'll try not to fall off the mountain. And if you see Sky cowering underneath that coffee table, get outside, because you'll only have a few minutes before things start to rattle. Between Sky and Pirate, I'd say you've got the two leading earthquake experts in Georgia."

"Mom, can we go have breakfast downstairs with Pirate? He's making pancakes! I can smell them," said Sierra.

"I'll take them down," I said.

"Get 'em dressed first!" Margie called out from the back bedroom. "Remember, we're going to Atlanta for some girl time today."

I changed into my running clothes and got the girls outfitted for their big-city adventure, and the three of us went down to breakfast together. Pirate had his buffet of delicacies spread over a six-foot-long fold-out table: coffee, Pop-Tarts, bagels, cream cheese, sausage, pancakes. Pickled eggs and pigs' feet in gallon jars decorated the center of the table—"for shock value," Pirate said; they looked like specimens in a mad scientist's laboratory. Hikers were circling the table with paper plates in hand, waiting for a new batch of pancakes. Pirate was doing what he loved best.

"Got a new batch coming in just a minute, folks. . . . Yeah, I'll sugar 'em up for you, no problem. . . . Anybody else for powdered sugar? Two, you said, or three?" He saw us coming down the steps and smiled.

"Allison! I have your favorite—pigs' feet," Pirate said, laughing as he picked up the jar. He swirled it a little and held it out to Allison, who ducked and grimaced, wrinkling her nose, playing the joke expertly for the benefit of the hiker audience waiting in line at the table.

"Okay, Pirate," said my little comedienne. "I'll try one more, but this is the last time."

The sun was starting to break over the mountains, revealing clear blue skies. Within an hour the ground frost would lift away, providing a perfect mixture of warmth and cool. I was ready to run the mountain.

The strenuous, 2.2-mile uphill run from the store to the summit of Blood Mountain has become my personal challenge. At 4,458 feet (and I know I am repeating myself), it is the highest point on Georgia's portion of the Appalachian Trail. My best running time is forty-two minutes. Today I will attempt thirty-five. Over the years, the staff has joined in the challenge; the staff record is held by a skinny-as-a-rail high-school cross-country runner named Winston Dangler, at twenty-eight minutes.

To me, the hardest part of running is the first quarter mile, when you have to put down the rebellion of your legs, ankles, knees, feet, head, heart, and lungs. The parts of the body are happy in their natural state, disconnected from one another, going through their automatic motions. Hard running forces them into communication, and the pain of that first quarter mile is like the pain of an awkward conversation. Brain tries to set Heart up with Lungs, but they don't hit it off. Joints get drunk and make inappropriate noises. Muscle sits alone in the corner and cries.

I cross the road to the Trail, and start my running ritual of setting my watch, checking the heart-rate monitor, adjusting the hose on my water pack, stretching my calves, and tightening up my headphones. I hit shuffle on the music player, having chosen one of my favorite albums: Van Morrison's *Poetic Champions Compose*. Track three, "Queen of the Slipstream," will start the morning pace. I set off.

I measure my steps to the rhythm of the music and to the map of the mountain that I keep in my memory. Sierra helped me draw this map; she has given names to special formations of rock and foliage along the Trail, names that only she and I know. The name-giving project started a few years ago as a game that we would play on our near-daily hike to climb on the rock faces near Balancing Rock.

I came up with the game as a way to teach her to look around and examine her surroundings, so that if she were ever lost or alone in the woods, she would find the clues that would help her get back home. It also served as a distraction against her minor complaints. But with time—when it seemed she had named half of the trees in the woods—the names took on a deeper meaning: they were part of how Sierra brought her world to life. Being in on the secret, knowing the names, we weren't just parent and child. We were friends; we shared an imagination. Every time I go past a certain root, I set my foot on it, for good luck. This is Rooty the Snake, a root that looks like a snake crawling on the ground. It's the first thing Sierra gave a name to, and the first landmark on the route.

After the first hundred yards, I enter a short, steep ascent, with a few tricky rocks, that eventually levels out at Alligator Rock, where the Trail flattens for the next hundred yards before it takes a sharp turn, just past the Sitting Tree, and sends me climbing again for another two hundred yards. In my head I hear Sierra's little voice, yelling for marshmallows, as I pass Happy Camp off my left shoulder. The memory fades back into the trees as I climb toward the Hollow Tree that sits on the right side of the Trail, with its snarled old roots trying to trip me up. Allison's voice now enters my head. Her vocabulary has gotten bigger and her sentences longer, and she now hears and sees everything. Daddy, isn't that Sissy's pee-pee rock?

My body is now starting to communicate openly among all its parts and pieces. The conversation is beginning to go more smoothly. The heart monitor reads 140. I'm entering my "zone," the point where my limbs at last catch on to the rhythm of my blood and breath, and my legs become, like my heart, things that move without having to be asked. This is a beautiful feeling, as long as it lasts. I hang on to it for the next half mile, passing Turtle Rock, Bear's Hole, and Balancing Rock before entering the leg-burning section just past the Freeman Trail intersection. I check my watch. Twelve minutes. One mile in, and I'm ahead of schedule.

But the mountain punishes optimism. Within moments, my heart rate has left the zone and gone shooting past 160, as I climb the first steep set of stone stairs. I grab for the CamelBak hose and force some water down my throat. The next few hundred yards allow me to get the heart rate into the bearable 150 range. I use my arm to wipe some sweat from my dripping forehead, and my better

Felicity's son romps in front of Mountain Crossings on a warm, late-winter day.

judgment screams at me for wasting energy with such a thing. I am begging Van Morrison for an upbeat song before I enter the Stupid Stairs—the steepest set of all, certain to send my heartbeat above 170 and set my quad muscles aflame—when instead I get "Give Me My Rapture":

> *There are strange things happening every day*
> *I hear music up above my head*
> *Fill me up with your wonder*
> *Give me my rapture today*

The song is a teasing invitation to look up and find that music above; it appeals to the easygoing sightseer in me. I have to force my eyes down. Watch the feet; don't look up. Rapture comes later. I turn inward toward the music and listen carefully to the next line.

> *Let me contemplate the presence so divine*
> *Let me sing all day and never get tired*
> *Fill me up from your loving cup*
> *Give me my rapture*

I think Van and I might agree about a few things, but I have no extra breath for singing, so I turn my focus beyond the words and onto the Celtic instrumentals. It helps. I push through the pain in my legs, willing more air into my lungs, and with a final effort I reach the top of the Stupid Stairs. My run becomes a ragged shuffle as I try to lower my heart rate. A subtle incline gives me just the break I need to grab some water and rinse out my mouth. Another sharp turn happens at Barney's Tail—a switchback that a very young Sierra named for her favorite dinosaur. Water has muddied the Trail here. The sight of it makes me feel cooler.

Another set of smaller stone stairs climbs just ahead. They're not big enough or bad enough to have a name, but they still serve a dose of pain to the already-burning legs. Above the stairs I enter a maze of boulders and crooked stones that like to eat ankles. I hop over them along my practiced path. Once on the other side, the Trail drops down a few feet before taking an equal rise up and onto a three-hundred-yard flat section that leads toward an open rock face known to hikers as Wrong-Turn Vern. It's the biggest dogleg on this route and is known for deceiving northbound hikers who are descending the mountain and don't see the hard left turn or the white marker painted on the speckled, gray granite. Hikers who miss this turn will follow the rock face downhill a few hundred feet before they even start suspecting the error. I make the turn and pass under a canopy of oaks, hemlocks, and white pines that stretches 150 yards along a wide, sandy trail bed with a slight incline that leads me to a tunnel of rhododendron. My heart rate has dropped to a tolerable 145, back into the zone.

The rhododendron scent—like a mix of nutmeg and honeysuckle—is strong this morning. The flowers of the rhododendron are still sleeping, waiting for warmer temperature to call them forth. Frost still hangs on the leaves, and they offer a sweet, refreshing relief when they brush gently across my face as I push through. On the other side of the tunnel is another granite face. *Go fifteen feet to the left, and it's easier but a few steps longer. Face it head-on, and it's shorter but steep, nearly impossible if it's wet. Today it's dry. Take it on.* I charge onto the harder route before I can change my mind and come out upon a rock face that commands one of the views I live for: the Georgia Appalachians all around, under sheets of lifting mist, wearing by the morning light that blue-gray-green that belongs to no other mountains.

Here the unknowing often think they have reached the top. I see two enjoying the morning sunrise right now: young lovers sitting on the rock face, cuddled together beneath a red fleece University of Georgia blanket. The girl sees me first. She apparently assumes that I am going to stop, and when I pass them she calls out, looking bewildered, "Sir, is this the top?" My mouth is dry, my lungs are near empty, and my heart is pumping at 163 beats a minute. All I can say is "No!"—even this expenditure of breath hits me like a stab—as I go puffing into the second tunnel of rhododendrons. This time the smell is bitter, and the leaves don't feel so gentle. Their soft brushes have become harsh slaps, and I must be wearing down. I'm arguing with myself.

That girl asked you a simple question, and you don't have the courtesy to stop and give them directions to the top. That's just rude; your mother taught you better than that. You should go . . . Would you just shut up? I'm trying to make thirty-five.

I punch out of the second tunnel and see a thread of smoke rising from Sierra's favorite campsite. A purple tent the size of a truck is set up just beyond. A black labradoodle appears from behind the tent, barks three times, and then changes its tune into a screaming howl. A sleepy voice from inside the tent hollers, "Garbo! Quiet!" I pick up my pace and race for the third rhododendron tunnel. My heart, lungs, legs, and brain are starting to squabble. They don't want another big hill. Luckily there is none. I can no longer lift my arms to read the heart-rate monitor; my guess is 168. *Hey, old man—you need to drop that heartbeat to no more than 161 if you want to take on the last hundred yards at a full sprint. If you don't, that heart is going to black your ass out, and Garbo the labradoodle will have you for breakfast.* I turn to some guidance from ol' Van and try to concentrate on the next verse of "The Mystery":

Let go into the mystery, let yourself go
You got to open up your heart, that's all I know
Trust what I say and do what you're told, baby
And all your dirt will turn into gold

Finally, some advice I can use. My heart is slowing down—letting go, opening up—as I move past the third tunnel and pop out the other side onto the last granite face before entering into a concluding tunnel that leads to my official destination, Blood Mountain Shelter. I will my legs to expand their stride; I force my back up straight in an effort to open my lungs. I race across the granite top. I smell smoke from a nearby fire and tell myself it's the rubber burning on the soles of my shoes. I sprint into the last thicket, which is a mix of smaller white oaks and rhododendrons—the dirt path is wider and firmer here. I can see the old stone wall of the shelter; the pains melt away, and I am now in full stride within yards of the finish line. I reach the south corner of the building, but must completely pass it to officially stop the clock. I throw my chest out, my head forward, and hit my mark, then tumble immediately to the black, ashen dirt before the opening of the shelter, where the scent of campfires gone by is for me the smell of victory. I roll onto my back, lift my left arm, and push the button to stop my timer, but I am too tired to look at my time.

I lie there, flapping my arms and legs in the dirt like a kid making snow angels. I hear my heart pounding in my chest. I can even feel it vibrating the earth. As the endorphins flood my head, there's a euphoria of being lifted onto a fence line separating one universe from another—as though I'm sitting, teetering, and swinging one leg in each world. I delight in the view from this balancing act, this sensation of being between worlds, and enjoy the peace and quiet of the surrounding forest. The sky is clear blue, and there's a cardinal jumping among new, green leaves on a limb of the white oak that rises above the shelter.

My silence is broken by a familiar voice echoing against the rocks.

"You look like crap! Would you like some breakfast? I got extra oatmeal, but I'm out of Snickers bars. You wouldn't by chance have one in that water pack of yours, would you?"

I lift my head from the ground and see the skinny frame attached to the familiar voice standing in the shadowy doorway of the old stone shelter.

"Bumblefoot, if I could lift my leg high enough, I would kick you in the ass with it," I kindly tell him. I move my foot off the ground a few inches and slam it back down, raising a little dust.

"Oatmeal it is. Want some coffee to go with that, sweetie?"

"Sure. Sugar and cream please, honey."

"What was your time?"

"Oh, I forgot to look, had to be thirty-two, thirty-three."

I wipe the dirt off the face of my digital watch and punch a couple of buttons. "Here it is. My record time is . . . forty-three? What? That just can't be!"

Billy laughs and pours coffee. "That ain't so bad," he says. "I knew a one-legged blind man, about four-and-a-half feet tall, who dreamed his whole life about running this mountain in forty-three."

"Yeah, right," I groan, scowling at the watch. "This damn thing must be broken. I was flyin' up this mountain. If it weren't for the lovebird asking me questions back there or that howling labradoodle that tried to kill me, I would've made it."

"Labradoodle? What the hell is a labradoodle?"

When I arrive back at the shop, Buddy has just opened the store, and Felicity is walking through the front door followed by a line of hikers.

Groovy approaches me along the gravel pathway. She's wearing an old canvas pack attached to a wooden frame. I recognize it as a Trapper Nelson's Indian Pack Board, a standard issue for United States Forest Service employees back in the 1930s. Groovy's pack is well used, held together by various patches she must have collected through her years of travel. It isn't a pretty piece of equipment, but it's neatly packed and not at all overloaded. She has changed her look for hiking. Her gray hair is pulled back into a ponytail and tucked under a nylon ball cap, and the plastic sunflower is now pinned to the bill of the hat. She's wearing seventies-style running shorts—the kind with the drastic high cut in the hem—and red-on-white striped tube socks pulled up all the way to her knees; a black sports bra has replaced the photo T-shirt. Modesty is for the young, I guess. At least her footwear is current.

She waves me down. "Mr. Porter, can I talk with you for a moment?"

"Certainly. How can I help?"

"It's about the twins. I'm a little worried about them. They seem to be good kids, but something's just not right. If those kids are nineteen, then I'm nineteen, too. And you can plainly see that is not the case."

She makes a sweeping gesture over her body with her hands. She is, indeed, a long way past nineteen. I don't know how to comment on this. My mouth hangs open for a moment until she resumes her speech.

"They say that their parents told them not to tell anybody their last name or where they were from. Now, don't you think that's just a little strange? I think they're runaways."

I tell her that strange is something we get a lot of around here.

"Would you mind talking to them?"

"Is that them, coming up the stairs from the hostel?"

Groovy is right; nineteen seems to be a stretch for these two boys. They're identical from the tops of their short, butterscotch-blond heads to the tips of their white Nike shoes: thin, mischievous-looking, and gawky. The packs on their backs look as if they weigh as much as the boys and appear only slightly shorter than they are. Each step they take looks like a circus balancing act and requires total concentration on their part to keep the entire load from toppling. If they fall forward, they'll be crushed; if they fall backward, they'll be stuck like upside-down turtles. Their blue jeans have holes in the knees, and they both wear faded white dress shirts one size too large. They look more like a set of homely Mormons on a mission than runaways.

With her smooth, quiet voice, Groovy makes the introductions. "Brandon, Braden, I want you to meet Mr. Porter. He is the owner here, and he may be able to help you with those packs."

"Welcome to Mountain Crossings, guys. First, how am I supposed to tell you apart?"

"I'm Braden, sir. I'm the oldest by an hour and a little taller by a half inch."

"I'm Brandon, sir. Yes. A little shorter. But my mouth isn't always running like my brother here."

"That's not much to go on, but I guess I'll figure it out. How far are you two headed?"

Braden serves as the spokesman, while Brandon steps back slightly behind his brother.

"Not sure," he says cautiously. "We have three months."

"By the looks of that travel luggage on your back, it appears that you have the entire three months packed on the inside and outside."

"No, sir. Our mom is bringing some more food in about four weeks."

"Four weeks; no kidding? Where does your mom have to drive from?" I ask, testing Groovy's comment about them not telling where they are from.

"Well, sir, we aren't allowed to say," Braden says sheepishly.

It is clear that these two don't trust strangers. I choose not to push the point further and decide to wait and build some more credit before trying to bring down the wall of mistrust.

"Braden, Brandon, I am really going to try hard to not sound like your daddy. By the looks of those packs and all the stuff hanging off of them, along with the cotton clothing you're wearing—quite simply, men, you are unprepared. If you two continue with some of that shit you have stuffed in your luggage, then there is a good chance you could have a near-death experience, or worse, in these woods. Hopefully, the last five days have been humbling and that has opened your ears up a little. If you two are willing to listen, then I can help you."

Like abandoned ducklings who have found a surrogate mother, Brandon and Braden both look to Groovy for the answer. She picks up on the cue. "I think that you should listen to Mr. Porter here; I've been hiking these trails a long time, and you two could really get yourself in trouble."

"Yes, ma'am."

"Yes, ma'am."

They both drop their shoulders and nod their heads in unison and start the twenty-four-step climb up the stairs toward the shop, wobbling under the weight of the packs.

Sometimes you see where a trail name is going to come from before you know exactly what the trail name is going to be.

"Groovy, are those wheels on the bottom of those packs?"

"Yes. Over the past five days they have been carrying and rolling those bags across the Trail."

Just then, I spy Alpine walking down the pathway headed for the trash bin with a Santa Claus–sized sack of garbage. He detours over and greets me with a concerned look on his face.

"Winton, there's this guy—he's been here for about three days. I think he's living up in the woods."

"Is he the one missing his right hand?" I ask him. "Carrying a rolled-up, yellow blanket around his back? Wearing a daypack and toting a duffel bag?"

"Yes. That's him."

"Yeah, he is a little hard to miss. Where is he at now?"

"I think he's still on the balcony digging in the garbage can."

We call them duffel-bag hikers. Every year we get about a half dozen of them. They either know about the Trail or tripped onto it by accident on their way to somewhere else. They assume that they can simply blend into a community of long beards and dirty people. They have little or no money or food, and typically the only clothing they own is what they are wearing, which is usually all cotton. Sometimes they are avoided or shunned by hikers, but the generosity of many hikers runs deep. Partly out of goodness, partly out of pride, hikers want to help; they want to teach others what they know. They might offer advice, then a listening ear, and then eventually food or money. The duffel-bag hikers, like stray dogs, will keep following the food until a more generous benefactor comes along or they realize that they have worn out their welcome.

This one we call Lefty, because the left is the only hand he has. A gaunt, tormented-looking man in his late forties (though it's hard to tell), skinny as a weasel, his face all knobby bones, Lefty has a black-as-ash beard and wears an ancient, filthy Atlanta Flames cap over an untidy bird's nest of hair sticking out on all sides. I find him on the balcony as described, bent over the rim of a trash can and peering around inside, looking for whatever Alpine missed. He tries smiling at me pleasantly, like one neighbor to another, as though digging in the trash were simply a nice thing to do on a spring morning.

"Nice ball cap," I say. "I haven't seen one of those in over twenty years. Are you okay? Can I help you in any way?"

"Well, I really need to get to Western Union and pick up some money."

My experience with the duffel-bag hikers has led me to always look for a window of opportunity that will help speed the process of moving them away from the Trail and toward the safer ground of a small town or Greyhound bus station. This opportunity comes quickly this morning. I tell him I am heading toward town and could get him at least halfway; I just have to check on the staff first.

I step into the store and find the twins going over the candy racks as though they were choosing melons at a grocery store—picking up, putting down, trying to find the perfect piece. Buddy is at the counter, processing a stack of outgoing UPS boxes filled with gear that hikers have packed for sending home. Felicity is listening to another story about a hiker's first bear encounter ("It's never happened to me before, I was a little scared, it was amazing, and you should've . . ."). And Jennifer is in today, for the first time in more than a month, and in the bliss of new love she looks every bit as dopey and distracted as Alpine. She would call it sweeping the floor, what she and the broom are doing, but it is more like pairs figure skating—just a series of fluttering twirls. I check the top layer of sticky-note messages on my desk in the back, find nothing urgent, grab two cups of coffee, and go back to the door—dodging Jennifer as she glides by with the broom, smiling at empty space.

I tell Buddy I am giving a guy a quick ride down the mountain and will return in a few minutes, and he finds a place in his stream of muttered complaints for a reply. "What's with these people? Don't people know how to write anymore? I can't read this label. Screw it. I don't care if the damn thing ends up in China. Okay, boss!—later! How do they expect me to read this? There are chickens that write better than this."

Lefty is waiting at the bottom of the stairs. I hand him the cup of coffee and point him to the old Toyota Previa van. I open the front door, which causes the alarm in the car to go off. Lefty drops his duffel bag and jumps back from the vehicle as if trying to distance himself from the possible crime.

"No worries, it does this all the time," I tell him. Before the car will start, I have to pop the hood, disconnect the battery to disarm the alarm, then reconnect it. "There. That should do. Jump on in; she won't blow up now. It was the red wire. Snip, snip."

I don't know why I say things like this, by the way. Somehow it reassures me, living among the strangest of the strange, to know that I have enough strangeness of my own to keep people off balance. Poor Lefty is beginning to suspect that I'm crazier than he is. Touching the handle of the van door as though it's a hot skillet, he steps up and slides onto the passenger seat. I start the van, pull to the end of the driveway, and wait for three slow-moving logging trucks to pass by before entering the roadway. It's going to be a long ride down with these things in front of me. I pull in behind them and tilt my right foot toward the brake pedal.

"Well, how did you end up at the Mountain Crossings store?" I ask my passenger.

Lefty's not used to having company, so chitchat requires great concentration. He knits his brows, and I feel for him. "Well, man, you know, like, I wanted to go to a national forest, you know; they're, like, everywhere. Well, the sheriff down there in Dahlonega, friendly guy, was nice enough to drive me up here, you know, to your store."

My store is on the county line. What Lefty is saying is that the friendly sheriff was nice enough to drive him out of the sheriff's jurisdiction. Which is exactly what I'm trying to do, hoping that the next friendly sheriff will carry him to the next county line or, better, into North Carolina, fifteen miles away.

The logging trucks' brakes are starting to smell like burnt rubber, and they slow to a near crawl at the hard twist in the road next to Goose Creek Cabins. Lefty just looks away.

"Yeah, there are a lot of national forests," I say. "Have you ever hiked the Appalachian Trail?"

"The Appalachian Trail. Appalachian Trail? You know, I know I've heard of it. Now where is that at?"

"You were just on it. It goes all the way to Maine. Two thousand one hundred and seventy-eight miles."

That's a lot of rides from friendly sheriffs, he's probably thinking.

"No, I never did, but I'd like to. I got a little time on my hand," he says with a creepy smile while holding up his one good hand. I'm silent at this, long enough for him to worry that I haven't got the joke, so he repeats it. "I said, I got a little time on my hand."

"If you want to hike that Trail to Maine, you may want to make some adjustments on some of that equipment. The weather out there can be pretty unforgiving, and that little towel you call a blanket just ain't enough against what you could run into out there."

"I've been pretty warm over the past several days. I should be fine," he says.

"I hope so."

That's all there is to say, then. I don't know how he could pay for better equipment anyway.

We spend the next few minutes in silence as we inch our way down the road behind the logging trucks. Finally, where Georgia 180 splits off to the east from U.S. 19/129, I pull into a small gravel parking area. "Well, here you go. Just head north on that road, and you'll run into Blairsville."

"Okay, thanks for the ride. You wouldn't happen to have a couple of bucks you could loan me?"

I scoop up a handful of change out of the ashtray. Lefty holds up both arms, apparently forgetting that he has only one hand. He opens the one hand, and I dump the coins into his palm. He looks down at the change, his hand and stump still together, and gives a peculiar smile. It seems to contain both gladness at his new fortune and tender regrets for the hand that is missing. I have the impression that he sees two hands where I see only one. He steps away from the van and closes the door.

On the A.T., survival depends on water, warmth, and shelter.

CHAPTER SIXTEEN
Samsonite Twins

For thousands of years, this system of mountains, with its heavy forests and its endlessly succeeding ridges, has slowed and broken Atlantic storms; and for thousands of years, the same storms have gradually battered the Appalachians down, carving the eastern faces with slopes that resemble snowboarders' half-pipes, and gaps that will send winds blasting through like a spitball through a straw. Now and then, a wandering gust of Atlantic weather will meet some cold northwest air going the other way, and the valleys under Blood Mountain become again, as in legend, the scene of a battle: a battle between storms.

Today, after three days of bitter fighting, a freak Great Lakes blizzard has won a victory. Having already dumped hundreds of inches of snow from Minnesota to Kentucky, it has blanketed North Georgia with accumulations of four to eight inches, with reports of twenty-four inches in Great Smoky Mountains National Park, fifty-five miles north. It is late May, and temperatures have fallen below twenty degrees.

I have been up most of the night, putting antifreeze in toilets, checking on the many miles of water pipes, rotating electric heaters throughout the old building, and keeping the wood stove in the shop burning. Margie and the girls are huddled on the floor in the den of the house under a collection of old down sleeping bags. Sky, after making the first early rounds with me, decided that her services were better employed warming the feet of the children. When she hears me walk by, she does not lift her head, but rather peeks through one eye, as if to say: *Please, don't ask me to go outside again.* I tiptoe down the inside back stairs to the hostel—trying not wake Pirate, who is sleeping just below—and quietly unlock the door that opens into its common area. But Pirate is already awake. Before I can open the door, I find his hand on my shoulder.

"It's 4:30, Pirate. Why are you up so early?"

"Hell, I've been up for an hour. It's late now. Want some coffee?"

"Sure, but I didn't bring my cup."

"I got one. Let me wipe it out."

Pirate looks around the counter for a hand towel, a paper towel, a napkin, but can't find one quickly enough, so he uses his shirt to clean out the bottom of an old Barnum & Bailey clown cup that he grabs from the shelf. "There you go. That oughta work," he mumbles as he pours from the muddy coffeepot.

"How many we got in the bunks tonight?" I ask him, as I take a sip from my cup and feel the grains of coffee on my tongue and teeth.

"It's a full house. Good coffee, huh?"

"Yeah. Next time you really should use a filter. Are the twins here?"

"Yep. I had to put them on the floor last night. They were going to camp out, but I guess they changed their mind."

"Have you heard any more about the weather?"

"Yep. According to the radio, it should be over today and back to sunny skies and upper seventies by tomorrow."

"That's good. It should make this group a little happier today. Now, Pirate, I would love to stay and chew some more of this delicious coffee," I say with a grin and a tip of my cup, "but I have got to shovel some snow, salt the walkways, and throw some more wood on the fire in the shop."

When the sun is shining and there is no wind in the air, shoveling snow can be therapeutic. This is not one of those days. I hurriedly clear one side of the stairs with the snow shovel, creating a two-foot path to the shop, and toss salt crystals onto the stone walkway near the entrance. Then I slip into the store and lock the latch. I find old Iron Maiden burning bright, and her warm glow calls me over. I put another log inside her steel belly and take a seat in front in my old Lafuma fold-up recliner chair. The shop is quiet, but my head is not. . . .

Have I taken care of everything? What else needs to be done? Who did I help yesterday, and are they safe in this weather today? Where is Lefty? And what about the twins—will they listen, who are they, where are they from, are they runaways? I need to know. Do I want to know?

At some point, the internal chatter stops, and I fall asleep in my chair. I am awakened by a hard rattling at the door and the ringing of the phone. Iron Maiden is down to smoldering ash. The air is colder, and the morning light is pouring through the windows. In my groggy state, I crawl to the counter and pull myself up to my feet, uncertain which event deserves my attention first. I see through the window that Bumblefoot is the rattler of the door—he can wait, so I head for the cordless phone next to the cash register and answer it while walking to the door: "Mountain Crossings, this is Winton, how can I help you?" I unlatch the door and let Billy inside.

The voice on the phone is scratchy and keeps breaking up.

"What was that? Could you speak up? 'Let go' of what?"

"Not 'let go,' " Billy says, demonstrating his powers of interpretation. "*Lego.*"

"Lego?"

"Yeah! Winton! It's Lego! Can you hear me?"

"I hear you, Lego. What's happening?"

"There this guy!" says the anxious, broken voice on the other side. I can tell he is shouting, but he sounds far away.

"Lego, where in the hell are you? You'd better be in the woods, because the reception on that cell phone sucks."

"Can you hear me now?"

"Not really, dude. You still sound like you're at a rock concert."

"No, not Hawk Mountain! Blue Mountain! Blue Mountain Shelter!"

"I didn't say Hawk Mountain, I said rock con—"

"We're at Blue Mountain Shelter! And there's this guy! And! Well! We can't get him moving! He's cold! Wearing all-cotton everything! We can't get him moving! He refuses to let us help!"

"Let me guess. Is he in his midforties, carrying a duffel bag, and missing his right hand?"

"What?"

"I said, midforties, carrying a—"

"What?"

"His hand! His hand! Lego, is he missing his right hand?"

"Yes! How did you know?"

"Lucky guess. Does anybody there have some extra clothes? A jacket, blanket you can get on him?"

"No! Everything's wet and frozen! We got to get out of here!"

"Well, you can't just leave him there. Could you get me a pulse rate?"

"Huh?"

"Lego, check his pulse! Heart rate! Give me the number!"

"Okay! Hold on!"

The phone goes dead. Lego must have moved from his one square foot of reception. I hang up, and Billy hands me a cup of coffee from the other side of the counter, then leans on the counter while cradling his own cup in both hands.

"Good to be in the front row," he says.

I pick up the phone after one ring. "What you got, Lego?"

"We're getting sixty-five. Damn, it's cold. Man, we got to go."

"Lego, give me your cell phone number."

Lego calls out the number, and I repeat it out loud as Billy copies it into his little journal.

"Lego, listen. We will call rescue, but you got to get this guy moving. I don't care if you have to kick him down the mountain—get him moving. Head towards Unicoi Gap. It's two miles downhill. Do you understand me?"

"Yes, sir. Get him moving," Lego confirms. Then the line goes dead, with a soft hiss like the sound of snowfall.

"Union County 911. What is your emergency?"

"This is Winton Porter at Mountain Crossings. I got a call from a cell phone near Blue Mountain Shelter. There is a forty-five-year-old male, missing his right hand, about six feet, hundred sixty pounds; we're getting about sixty-five beats per minute. He's conscious and has symptoms of hypothermia."

"Where is that?"

"Two miles south, on the Trail above Unicoi Gap."

"Is that in Union County?"

"No. It's closer to Helen. I think that's White County."

"Well, sir. You'll need to call White County."

"Ma'am, I am just the middleman here, and this is the only phone number we have for emergency. Any chance you could make the phone call?"

Pause.

"Well. It's not how we usually do things, but I guess I can do that. Would you give me your name again?"

I repeat my name and give her Lego's phone number and wait, expecting further instructions, for what seems too long.

"Sir, did you say his name was Lego?"

"Yes, ma'am. I don't know his real name. That's his trail name. It's an alias."

"Trail name? Alias? And should I put down Winton for your real name or trail name?"

"No, that's my real name. Do you need anything else?"

"No, sir. Thank you."

"Thank you," I say and hang up the phone.

"Sounds like you didn't get rid of Lefty after all," Billy says.

Over the next hour, the store bustles with people trying to warm up and dry out while discussing the weather and equipment:

"What happened? It was near seventy degrees last week, and now this?"

"Global warming. I tell you: global warming, El Niño, that's what's happening."

"I spent a hundred and forty bucks on my twenty-degree down sleeping bag and nearly froze my ass off. Ridiculous."

"My fiberglass tent poles froze and shattered on my tent last night. Can you replace that? Can you fix that? I don't even know."

"Have you ever eaten frozen ramen noodles?" . . . and so on.

The twins circle the store, looking at all the gear for the hundredth time, then settle, as always, in the pantry, drooling over Pop-Tarts, candy bars, brownies, cinnamon buns, and potato chips, trying to determine what delectable treat they'll spend their daily money rations on today.

Presently I see Brandon walking around with a candy bar, following closely behind Braden, who has a bag of Skittles clutched tightly in his palm. They seemed to be arguing about each other's choice of candy. Brandon waves his Milky Way when he wants to make a point, and Braden rattles his bag of Skittles. They're either children playing at being adults or adults playing at being children.

"You don't need that, Braden. You bought a thing of Rolos yesterday. Put it back."

"I don't have to listen to you. It's my dollar, and I can do whatever I want with it."

They are so deeply embroiled in this dispute that they don't even acknowledge me when I walk up beside them.

"Ah, brotherly love!" I say. "That gives me such fond memories. Well, boys, have you thought any more about doing some work around here, earning some money so you can get your equipment right?"

Brandon's voice of anger changes to a quiet, politely respectful tone (this happens quickly, strangely—one mood mechanically replacing another, like the chambers of a revolver clicking into place) when he says, "Yes, sir. But we need to call our mother first and see if it is all right with her to do work in the yard. We have to call her today, anyway, and give her an update on our Bible studies."

I think to myself, "Call your mother? You're nineteen years old, or so you say. Why do you have to get permission? Update on Bible studies? I don't want to know the details of that right now."

But what I say is, "Okay, I understand. She's worried about you two using power tools. When you talk with Mom, would you let her know that I would like to talk with her, so I can tell her what you will be doing around here over the next week? Also, I found some used packs in storage that may fit the two of you, but we'll need to check the fit later."

It isn't until the fourth day after their arrival, following a lot more coaxing, that they finally let me go through their packs. Nearly all of the gear and clothing proves to be worthless. In addition to their Samsonite luggage travel packs, complete with wheels, they each have five pairs of jeans, six cotton T-shirts, eight pairs of cotton socks, one hooded sweatshirt, and, for rain protection, a dollar-store plastic poncho that looks like a cheap trash-can liner. They each have a set of steel pots (one-liter and two-liter), all as black as coal because they don't have a stove and are cooking over an open fire—which explains the fold-up metal grate they have taken turns carrying, strapped to the outside of their packs. They have a water filter and two water-filter straws that they say they found in the Springer Mountain Shelter. The filter doesn't work, and the filter straws never have worked. Their only maps are pages torn from a Rand McNally road atlas for Georgia and North Carolina. For reading material, they have four pounds of religious stuff. They share a four-person tent that weighs exactly nine and a half pounds and must be ten years old, but smells like twenty. Pirate takes an academic interest in their sleeping bags, which, at five-plus pounds each, remind him of the bag he'd been issued in Vietnam thirty-five years ago. They don't have sleeping pads.

Rather unexpectedly, a funny thing happens when I try to teach them something about their gear: they listen for maybe fifteen seconds, and then their attention, as though by reflex, just fixes itself to something else, anything else. They stare right through me, slack-jawed, the way a dog does when you've got a bone in your hand; they give me the feeling that I could sing and dance without their noticing. For instance, I try to tell them that sleeping pads help regulate body temperature: they work like insulation in a house, I say, and without them, your body heat will get sucked into the earth. They listen to this and nod, and I think we might be getting somewhere, but a moment later, as I try to continue, it happens again—they just change the channel. Brandon scratches his head and turns to stare at women's footwear; Braden yawns and studies the grain of the floorboards.

After a three-hour—yes, three-hour—shakedown, I feel something like embarrassment, as though I've been talking to myself all afternoon. I asked them to think about what we've "discussed"—this is a pretty generous word for our peculiar interactions—and decide what they want to work on solving first. They have an answer for me.

Brandon pushes some change across the counter for his candy bar and says with a glazed look in his eyes: "You know, Mr. Porter, we been thinking about it. I think our gear has been working okay. The only thing we could really use is a pocketknife. How much would that cost?" Braden scoots in a little closer to his brother and nods in agreement while tearing into his packet of Skittles.

"We can address weaponry later," I say. "For now, let's stay focused on keeping you alive in these woods."

It is difficult not to get angry at the earnest stupidity of these boys. It is twenty-eight degrees outside, and they've got a few pair of blue jeans. Our hostel is saving their lives even as we speak. A new pocketknife is the least of their worries, and I'm still not convinced that they're old enough to buy one without their mother's consent.

Besides, they have no money, and that's why we're talking about power tools. "Our mom gave us twenty bucks when she dropped us off at Amicalola, and I found a few coins on the Trail," Braden told me two days ago. What they need is clothing, better sleeping bags, a more reliable tent, and some non–carry-on backpacks. Or a bus ticket home, wherever home is.

"Winton, phone!" Buddy hollers, and he hands me the phone. "Some guy named Eggo."

I grab the phone immediately. "Lego, did you get him moving?"

"Yeah!" Lego shouts. "We got him moving! We're down here at Unicoi! And the guy's still refusing help! There must be six rescue vehicles here! And one of the biggest damn rescue helicopters I ever seen! I never seen one with wings on it! What? Winton? What? Are you there? I have a bad . . . "

Lefty survived. What I later found out was that rescue managed to convince him to get into the ambulance, which took him to the hospital, where he was treated for hypothermia. From there he was released, or escorted, or expelled, into North Carolina. The biggest helicopter Lego had ever seen was Emory University Hospital's multimillion-dollar Sikorsky S-92, dispatched all the way from Atlanta—evidently in the belief that the rescuers would have to deal with a trauma victim.

As for the supposed trauma victim, well, there's a chance that the misunderstanding began with me, when I told the emergency operator that the victim was "missing his right hand." Imagine the telephone game: missing his right hand, lost his right hand, a bear took his arm off. Next time, if there is a next time, I'll use the word "amputee."

In the end, Lefty was off the mountain, alive, and now out of the state of Georgia. The cost to the people of White County—the county that finally rolled snake eyes—for the vagabond's rescue and state-line extradition was estimated at more than $35,000.

We talked about that number in the shop for weeks, comparing estimates. Margie did some research and found out that White County could have bought Lefty a new prosthetic hand for less than $15,000. Buddy suggested a Greyhound bus ticket to New Jersey for less than a hundred dollars.

"Not that he'd last long in Jersey," Buddy added.

Outside, the flame azalea, purple spiderwort, and white mountain laurel are opening back up to enjoy the afternoon sun. Temperatures have shot into the fifties, and the snow has melted away completely from the stone walkways, the parking lot, and the roads. At the higher elevations, along the northern slopes of the Trail and in the shaded areas atop Blood Mountain, it may last one more day. . . .

Braden is playing with Allison in the front garden, trying to help her salvage the remains of a small, melting snowman. I'm on the front walkway, helping a hiker load up, watching Allison's tender efforts when I can. Brandon comes up to me from behind.

"Excuse me, Mr. Porter. We spoke to our mom, and she said that it would be all right to work here for a few days, but she did want to talk to you first. Here's her cell phone number. You can call her anytime."

I thank him and tell him I'll call in a few minutes.

Reading the phone number in my hand, I suddenly realize how little we know about these kids. Their accents tell us they're from the South. Their gear tells us that they don't know what they're doing. But we don't even know their last name. We asked them for it once. Braden replied that their father worked for Homeland Security, and that's why they couldn't tell us. We didn't ask again.

I step into the back room of the store and make the call. A woman answers.

"Hello, this is Winton Porter from Mountain Crossings. You asked me to call you."

"Oh, yes, I sure did. So happy to get a chance to finally talk with you. My name is Caroline, Caroline Patterson. The twins said you have been really nice to them. Thank you, bless you. Bless your heart."

She has a rich Southern tone in her voice. I imagine a big woman with big hair, wearing a yellow, flowered sundress, sitting in a rocker on her front porch, sipping sweet tea and listening to gospel music. I turn up my own accent a few notches to gain her confidence.

"Thankyama'am, I do appreciate that. I have truly enjoyed havin' these boys around the shop over the past week. But, ma'am—I really gotta be honest with you. If these boys keep on this Trail with all the junk they have on their backs, then they are going to get hurt out there. Now, we've managed to find several hundred dollars in used gear and equipment that will fix most of the problems, but they still need about four hundred dollars in new gear and clothing to make it right. I've told them that they could do some yard work around the shop and earn some credit for the equipment. But apparently they need your permission first."

"It's okay with me," she says. "How are they doin'? Are they takin' their medications?"

Outside, Allison throws a handful of slush at Braden and laughs when it splatters in his face. I have no idea if he's taking his medications.

Felicity Keddy and Nate's wife, Tina Helminiak, wear the store's spirit in their smiles.

CHAPTER SEVENTEEN
Double Dose

The population of the little town of Jesup—the seat of Wayne County in southeastern Georgia—is ten thousand–plus, of whom I had known only two. One was a college roommate I hadn't seen in more than fourteen years, and the other was a hiker named Joe Naia, the lead investigator for the Wayne County sheriff. The Mountain Crossings crew met Joe in early May 2001, when I was preparing to take over the store, and he was about fifty-five. He looked and acted about ten years younger. He had the build of a long-distance runner—thin and sinewy, no loose flesh; his weight probably had never varied more than eight pounds in his adult life. Joe was 30.7 miles into his lifelong dream of hiking the Appalachian Trail.

That day in 2001, I found Joe in the backyard of the shop trying to configure a shelter out of a huge blue construction tarp. A stranger to me then, he looked like a kid trying to lay a blanket on a windy beach: feet stretched out, hands grabbing for sticks and rocks to throw onto the corners he could not reach. When he got one corner held down, another would flap up. I enjoyed the clown performance for five minutes before approaching him on the hill.

"Don't you have a tent?" I said.

"I had a tent, but it fell off my pack somewhere on the mountain," said Joe, grunting.

"You look like you're playing a game of one-man Twister."

The man fell to the ground and onto his knees, reached out a hand, and smiled. "Hi. My name is Joe."

I shook his hand, gave my name, and asked if he was headed for Maine.

"Yep. That's my plan."

"Well, if you would like, I can help you set up that tarp, or you can come inside and take some space on the couch."

"I only have thirty bucks."

"Well, I guess you'll just have to forget about room service."

Joe stayed at the house for two days. We talked both nights until late in the evening, about gear, family, dreams, and hiking, as if we had known each other all our lives. Joe wasn't a broke or homeless hiker down on his luck—he was just cheap. Nearly every piece of equipment he had was from Walmart, and nearly all of it had failed on the first thirty miles of the Trail. The pack was blowing seams, the sleeping bag nearly killed him in the cold; the tent was, as he said, "happily lost." He was a good guy without much of an idea of what he was doing, but he was ready to learn.

His trail name was given to him on our deck by one of the Trail's great teachers, a person Joe thought was a broke, homeless hiker, down on his luck—a poor old guy who was carrying less than twelve pounds in a pack the size of a grocery bag. Joe discreetly asked me to break a twenty so he could give him a few dollars.

I grinned. "You want to give that skinny fellow over there with the long beard sitting at the picnic table some money."

"Yeah. Not much—five, ten bucks. He needs the money more than I do, and he seems like a nice guy. I tried to help him last night, showed him all the equipment that I had and where I got it. He gave me my trail name."

"Follow me. Did he tell you who he was?" I led Joe to the bookshelves by the bay windows.

"No. I think his trail name was—Thimble? Thimblewill?"

"Close."

I handed Joe a book with the man's picture on the cover and watched his eyes pop open in amazement. I explained that his charity might be wasted on the author of *Ten Million Steps,* by M. J. "Eb" Eberhart, trail name Nimblewill Nomad, who was one of the most famous and accomplished distance hikers in the world—and one of the most humble, generous, and thoughtful, too. Nimblewill was an optometrist before he sold everything he had and became the first man to walk from Key West, Florida, to Canada. He'd also walked the Continental Divide Trail, the Pacific Crest Trail, the American Discovery Trail, the Lewis and Clark; he'd walked from North Carolina to Cape Disappointment in Washington State. Nimblewill might have earned Joe's five dollars outright—just for having the patience to listen to Joe talk about every piece of equipment that he had in his fifty-pound pack, how much he'd paid for it at Walmart—but Nimblewill took it out of Joe by giving him a trail name instead.

That's how Joe Naia became Walmart Joe.

Were the Samsonite Twins taking their medications?

Caroline Patterson's question, earlier this day, a few years after my meeting with Walmart Joe, had caught me off guard. I hadn't seen any medications when I went through their packs, and, anyway, what medications? For what ailments? Were they diabetics, epileptics, or psychotics? Or did they just have allergies?

I had asked Caroline how I would know if the twins weren't taking their medications, and the conversation had developed this way:

"Well, they sleep a lot if they don't take the medication, and they're a little more . . . " Here, Caroline must have stopped to sip sweet tea, choosing a word, while I quietly panicked. A little more what? A little more what?

" . . . *mooooody,*" Caroline said. "Are they around any children?"

Who in the hell have I let onto my property and into my house? What monster is out there right now, playing with my daughter and my daughter's melting snowman?

I went to the back room and found Alpine talking with a customer. Covering the mouthpiece of the portable phone with my hand, I pushed my shoulder into Alpine's back, nearly slamming him into the customer in front of him. He turned, and with great seriousness in my eyes and with anger in my whisper, I said: "Soldier, go get my daughter and bring her inside now. That's an order!" Alpine followed the command without so much as an "excuse me," leaving behind a baffled customer with one shoe on.

I returned my focus to the phone and tried to remain calm. I needed more information. I told Caroline I had two girls, three and seven years old by that time.

"Oh, they won't hurt them," she said, matter-of-factly. "Did you notice the scar on Braden's neck?"

"No, I haven't seen it."

"Well, Brandon choked him so hard one time that one of his fingers went into his brother's neck. It's a pretty good-size scar."

Fascinating. You're a few sandwiches short of a picnic, lady. "And this medication they're on helps with these, uh, anger-management issues? What kinds of medication are they supposed to be taking?"

Alpine returned from his mission, delivered Allison, and went back to the customer he had abandoned moments ago. Allison asked me timidly, "Daddy, why did you want to see me? My snowman is melting. I don't think he will last much longer; can I go back outside?" I stooped, spread my hand across her tiny shoulders, and held her to my knee. "I just wanted to know where you were," I told her, cupping my hand over the phone's mouthpiece.

"Well, actually they have a couple different medications," Caroline was saying, "but, yes, the main one is for social purposes. They sure have come a long way over the past couple of years! You see, they've been living in and out of orphanages and foster homes most of their life. We adopted them when they were thirteen, and that is a hard age for kids. You see, Mr. Porter, if they weren't up there on that Trail, they would both be in jail right now."

"Jail! What did they do?"

"Nothing yet, but if they were here they'd be in jail."

There's my opening. "Where's 'here' for you, Caroline?"

"Jesup, Georgia," she sang. "We're about forty-five minutes southwest of Savannah, Georgia." Hm, I thought, she must lay a foot on her accelerator. I drive fast, but it would take me at least an hour. . . .

Polite kids. They look normal. Social medication. Jail. Choking. Scars. Are they around children? What level of crazy are we dealing with here?

Who do I know in Jesup, Georgia?

"Listen, Mr. Porter, I really appreciate you looking after the boys. Would you mind getting a list of everything that you think they need? I can't come up this week, but I can next week, and I can stop by Walmart on the way up, but I will have to talk with their father first. I've got to go now."

"Caroline—just one more question. The boys say they're nineteen. Is that true?"

"I know they don't look it, but yes, they are nineteen. I must go; I can't talk right now; I will call you in a few days," she said anxiously, and hung up.

Stop by Walmart, she said. That's when I remembered who I knew in Jesup.

Joe is originally from New Jersey, where he started his career as a police officer and later became a detective for the New Jersey State Police. After thirty years of chasing murderers, gangsters, and drug dealers, the divorced father of two grown girls moved south, on his own. Unlike most Jersey retirees I've met on the Trail, he didn't make it all the way to Florida.

During one of our late-night talks, he described his life in Jesup this way: "I bought a house, sixty acres on a lake, a fishing pole. And what I found out in a relatively short time was that I loved to fish, but retirement bored me." The sixty acres was actually an old campground with fifty RV hookups, a couple of one-room cabins, and another fifteen basic campsites, which brought him a modest income to supplement his pension. After a year of fishing, mowing fields, and picking burnt beer cans out of fire rings, Joe decided to get more involved in the community. He started hanging out at the local doughnut shop and the barbecue joints, and he began accepting invitations from strangers to watch the baseball games of kids he didn't even know. Anybody who hadn't pulled a gun on him, Joe liked. A solitary retired life wasn't for him.

Eventually, one of his new friends in Jesup asked him to come to work for the sheriff's department. And that's where I find him today, three years after I last spoke with him. The tattered business card he'd given me was still in my wallet.

"Wayne County Sheriff's Department. How may I direct your call?"

"Captain Joe Naia's office, please."

"Hold one moment, please. I will transfer you."

"Hello, Sheriff's Office, how can I help you?"

"Is Captain Joe Naia available, please?"

"Can I tell him who is calling?"

"This is Winton Porter at Mountain Crossings, a shop on the Appalachian Trail," I say, knowing that the last part would not go unnoticed. No one in his department would have escaped a tale about the sheriff's captain hiking the Appalachian Trail.

"Appalachian Trail, of course. One moment please."

Soon I hear Walmart Joe's friendly shout. "Mr. Porter, how are you doing?"

"Joe, it's been a long time. I was wondering if you'd remember me."

"Never could forget you, Winton. You gave me shelter, bed, and food. You know, it's funny you called just now. You would have missed me if you'd tried in a couple of weeks—I'm headed for the PCT! I fly into San Diego, and . . ."

Joe is excited to talk to a trail person, someone who understands his obsessions. He goes on for several minutes, rarely taking a breath, telling me about his hopes of hiking the Pacific Crest Trail, recounting some of the highlights of his hike on the A.T. Eventually, he pauses to take a breath. I tell him I need his help.

He chuckles softly. "How can we help you here in Jesup, Mr. Porter?"

"Do you know the Patterson twins, Brandon and Braden, that live somewhere in Jesup? And are they in some kind of trouble?"

"No, that name doesn't ring a bell. It would have only come across my desk if they were involved in a felony."

I give Joe a short history of the Samsonite Twins and a summary of the conversation I had with their mother. I end my spiel with, "It sounds like if the local police don't know them, the pharmacy will."

"Wait a minute. Yeah. I know Brandon and Braden. They're up there with you. . . . Well, I know the parents better; I've only met the twins once or twice."

"Yes. Is that bad?" I ask.

"No. Those kids are in the best place they could possibly be, up there with you on the Trail."

"Their mother said the same thing. I wonder if one of you would mind explaining what the hell you mean."

"I mean, it'll do them some good. Fresh air, exercise. They need that. They're not bad kids. They don't have an easy time fitting in, but I don't think they're crazy. Typical teenagers. As for the parents, I don't know what to say. They're crazy, if anyone is. I somehow remember them calling us about the twins breaking into their barn and wanting us to arrest the boys and throw them in jail for the night."

"Why?"

"Apparently the family has a barn that the kids are not allowed to go into, and the boys kept breaking into the damn thing, so they called us and wanted them arrested. Typical teenage stuff. Don't know of any serious crimes they have committed."

"What's in the barn?"

"Don't know. We need a warrant for that," Joe says, and I get the feeling that he's just a bit more amused by this than I can afford to be. "I wouldn't worry about them, though. Being up there with you and away from here may just save their lives. I'll do some checking and see if there is anything we need to know."

"Please do. Apparently these kids are on enough medication that it could turn a horse into a lumbering cow. Or they're supposed to be. According to Caroline, as long as they take the meds, we should be fine. But I'm a little concerned that if they miss a dose or two we could have a horror flick in our future."

"Let me see what I can find out. I'll get back with you later, but I got to run for now. I'll call you back."

Joe hangs up the phone.

Later that day, I'm standing by the fireplace, deep in thought—wondering about that barn, whether it's full of livestock or pipe bombs, imagining the hoes, the barbed wire, the pitchforks—when I hear a childlike voice from behind say, "Mr. Porter, excuse me." I turn, and one of the twins is standing there, his shirt covered in mud, holding a shovel. He stands like a soldier at attention, expecting further directions of some sort; he has just accomplished something with the shovel. I step back, startled, pinning myself to the hearth.

"Mr. Porter, I am almost done planting those flowers in the garden. Do you want me to put some along the walkway?"

"Ha ha!" I say. "You're fast, man! I'd forgotten I asked you to do that. Thanks, Braden. No, you're Brandon. That would be fine, Brandon. Where's your brother?"

"I'm Braden. I don't know where Brandon is. I think he's taking a nap in the hostel."

"Your mom told me about your medication. What did she call it?"

"It's Hal-Oh, she calls it Hal-Oh. It keeps me focused on my studies."

"Oh. Well she asked me if you were taking it. Are you?"

"Yeah. I forgot yesterday, but I took some this morning."

"What about your brother?" Taking a nap? Did he take a nap yesterday? Did he take a nap the day before?

"I don't know," Braden says, yawning hugely. "You have to ask him. He doesn't like it much. Says it makes him shaky. Do you want me to empty the trash cans, too?"

"Yeah, that will be good."

Braden turns and goes out with his shovel—doing a stiff-legged march, with the shovel against his shoulder, which is either funny or insane—and I sneak to the window and watch him make a few trips back and forth to the garbage hutch. I find myself watching him with a detective's eye, a forensic attentiveness that makes me feel sort of silly. I'm trying to figure out where the crazy gene is hiding, exactly.

The medication. That's the next place to look. Once I know what "social medicine" Mom was talking about, I'll probably feel better, and then maybe I could relax a little more. The mother didn't give me the name of the medication, but Braden gave me a clue. I head for the computer and try a few Google searches: *hal oh medication, halo drug, haloh drug, halo crazy drug.* Eventually—how Google does this, I don't know—Google helpfully assumes that I've been trying to type *Haldol.* I click the top link anxiously.

The Web page comes up. There's a diagram of a molecule. Maybe it's like Ritalin for attention deficit disorder or Prozac for depression, or a B-vitamin supplement, something like that, no big deal; you could feed it to your—

SCHIZOPHRENIACONNECTION.NET

HALDOL ORAL

Haloperidol is used to treat certain mental/mood disorders (e.g., schizophrenia, schizoaffective disorders). This medicine helps you to think more clearly, feel less nervous, and take part in everyday life. It can also help prevent suicide in people who are likely to harm themselves. It also reduces aggression and the desire to hurt others. It can decrease negative thoughts and hallucinations.

Buddy, unloading some Snickers bars into the case behind the counter, sees me staring intently at the information on the computer screen. He takes a peek over my shoulder.

"You're tryin' to figure out how to get rid of those voices in your head, aren't you? I had the same problem; even went to the doctor," he says with a chuckle. "Doc told me that all I needed to do was get a divorce, and the voice in my head would probably go away. That was my first wife, and Doc was right. The voices went away, along with the car, house, furniture, the dog. . . ."

"Thanks for the advice, Buddy. But I am just doing a little research on the twins."

"I wouldn't worry about them. They're good kids, well mannered and relatively quiet. And they're not married to my first wife. How crazy could they be?"

The Samsonite Twins stay another week and a half before Mom finally shows up. Walmart Joe does call back and confirm that there are no outstanding warrants for Brandon and Braden. "Typical teenagers," he says. He also lets me know that he ran into Caroline in the grocery store a few days after we talked. He said that the look on her face when he told her that he and I were friends and had talked about the boys was "priceless."

I feel stuck. I don't know what to do. Part of me wants to drive them as far away from my family and my business as possible. I am consumed by the situation and try to find the answer from the staff, the winds, the trees, and the old building over a period of several days. I imagine a sneaky scheme to get rid of them: I will knock the boys out with a big dose of Xanax in their breakfast cereal, and then haul them away to Murphy in the van, leaving them passed out, with notes safety-pinned to their shirts, on the steps of the Cherokee County Courthouse. I try to imagine forgiving myself for this, but I can't.

In the end I guess the answer does come. Margie invites them into our home, lets them eat at our table, and eventually the twins open up and are leading the dinner conversation; at times we cannot shut them up. The twins are smart, and together their intelligence borders on genius. It turns out also that they are unusually well read, and they take turns citing passages from the works of Hemingway, Fitzgerald, Proust, and their favorite, Mark Twain. I ask if they have ever read Tolstoy. "*War and Peace*? *Anna Karenina*?" They both nod, at both books, and Braden is the one who says: "Now *that* man is crazy."

Cooking is the twins' hidden talent. They want to show their appreciation for our help, and for days they talk about cooking us a meal. At first we are hesitant. A vision of the haloperidol molecule flashes before my eyes, and I don't want them playing with knives in the kitchen. I am also afraid, given the potent pharmaceuticals they are packing, that they will drug us. We compromise and let them cook breakfast for the hikers and the staff. I give them fifty dollars, and Margie drops them off at the Ingles grocery in town and lets them shop. The next morning, they are up at 5 a.m. preparing breakfast, with knives and flame and all, in our kitchen. How they got into the house, I don't know.

Beyond the usual "good morning" salutation on my early rise to get a cup of coffee, they hardly speak a word during the entire process. They are two people working as one to get a meal prepared for nearly twenty people. They move Pirate's table into the breezeway, cover it with a white tablecloth, and replace the centerpiece of pickled pig feet and eggs with two candle lanterns and a vase full of the flowers that Braden planted the week before. They have a second table in the corner with a two-burner Coleman stove and two Teflon camp skillets where they can cook omelets on demand. The table is filled with an incredible array of foods—crêpes, fresh bananas, strawberries, melon, powdered sugar, boiled eggs, poached eggs, scrambled eggs, sausage, bacon, grits, cabbage, biscuits that sit in tins on top of Sterno cans. When it is over, they clean for two hours, washing every dish, fork, and spoon, and scrubbing every countertop and floor.

Eventually, Caroline does show up, four days later than promised. She isn't quite as I've imagined her. Although she does have big hair, she is thinner than her voice had led me to guess, and I'm not expecting the five-year-old and the twelve-month-old who come with her. She introduces herself with all of her Southern pleasantries.

"*Soooooo* nice to finally meet you! Thank you for taking care of my boys. God will bless you, and I'll keep you in my prayers."

She is anxious to lead me to her car so she can show me all the wonderful treats she brought for the boys. Her little Mercedes station wagon is stuffed full, and when she opens the hatch, various cans of vegetables and meats roll onto the pavement. Brandon dutifully picks up the cans, tosses them back into the car, and returns to a position behind me and to my right so they can still see the goodies in the car. Caroline seems to be one of those mothers who has conditioned herself in the world of "hurry-up." Unlike her telephone personality, she thinks fast, talks fast, and moves fast, and never in unison. She starts pulling the food out of the bags and laying it on the ground in the parking lot as if she needs my immediate confirmation or blessing. She holds up a CVS bag and shakes it a few times, rolls her eyes, and says, "This is one of the reasons I'm late. It took me nearly an hour to get the refills the boys needed for the next month, but I got 'em!"

I ask her if she's gotten the list of things I sent in an e-mail.

"*Weeeeell,*" she says, "*mooooost* of it. I had a chance to talk to the boys

The A.T. emblem welcomes anyone passin' thru at Mountain Crossings at Walasi-Yi.

after we talked, and they thought that their sleeping bags were going to be okay, but I did get them shorts and of course some more socks, but I couldn't find any of those wicking socks you told me about."

"What did you get?"

She reaches into the car, holds up two bundled six-packs of white cotton socks, and proudly proclaims: "Five ninety-nine at the dollar store! Here you go, boys—one for you! And one for you!"

"Caroline," I say with some disgust, "why don't you carry this mountain of gifts down to the hostel and spread it out on the floor. I feel confident that they won't be able to carry all of this out of here. I can meet you downstairs in a few minutes, and we can sort through it all."

"That would be fine, but I really wanted to take the twins down to town and get them something to eat. Could we do it later?"

"That would be nice, but it's 5:30 now, and I have a date with two little girls to go hiking. If you want my help, the dinner in town will have to wait."

She is annoyed with my response, but she agrees. While Caroline plays with the restless baby, the twins unload the groceries, sheepishly. (I gave them a stern look when Caroline mentioned their sleeping bags, and they haven't met my eye since.) Josh, the five-year-old, is excited to see his older brothers. The entire time, he stays within feet of both Brandon and Braden. He scampers after them, and they give him small things to carry.

Downstairs, the boys spread the food out across the floor and onto the couch. They are enjoying a bag of cookies when I step inside. Caroline is rocking the now-fed baby to sleep in a carrier on the floor.

"Well, boys," I say. "I am going to make this fast. We spent a lot of time together over the past weeks. First, I have some sleeping bags that will replace your old ones. I will bring those to you tonight. Also, you both grab two pairs of socks off the wall at the shop in the morning. You can save the new ones for college next fall. I will sort out enough food to get you to the Nantahala Outdoor Center, which is seven days from where you will get dropped off tomorrow. Caroline, I will give you directions to Dick Creek Gap, near Hiawassee, in the morning."

"Why can't they just start here?" asks Caroline.

I give the answer to the boys. "Brandon, Braden, no offense; you have both played the role of model children for three fun weeks, but I want you far enough away that you aren't tempted to walk back. Is that a good-enough reason?"

They yessir me solemnly.

"Caroline, when we are done sifting through the food, you will have to decide what you want to do with the other eighty-five percent. You can drive it or ship it to the Nantahala Outdoor Center, whatever works for you."

Caroline and the twins stay silent, while I quickly toss seven days' of food into one big pile on the floor. I don't tell them what is breakfast, lunch, or dinner, and in less than ten minutes I am done. I stand up and study the expressions on the twins' faces. They know that our friendship and the all-expenses-paid vacation at Mountain Crossings are coming to an end.

"*Bon appétit*," I say. "You have food for two for seven days. We have shown you how to pack the bag, set up the tent, and work your stove. You're lighter, more organized, and better educated. You crawled in here from Amicalola three weeks ago; now it's time to walk, boys. I'll see ya when I see ya."

They don't venture to say when that might be, and I don't ask them what was in the barn. We have found a kind of understanding.

Even without Baltimore Jack himself sitting behind the counter, regulars would recognize his signature "jack" bottle.

CHAPTER EIGHTEEN
Swingers in the Crosswinds

Long before Mountain Crossings became my home, it was the home—the *o-we-nv-sv*—of the Cherokee. They worshipped on this mountain, survived on its bountiful supply of food, and bathed under the 105-foot cascade of Nottely Falls—located less than five hundred yards away on the northern slope below my shop, but still hidden from today's crowds of tourists and hikers. The Cherokee considered the mountain a vortex of spiritual energy and the home of the Cherokee Wind Walkers. (According to lore, it was their job to hang the moon every night.)

It has been said that the energy that moves through the streams, the grasses, the leaves of the old oaks, the pines, and the locusts is like a centrifuge for harmonizing the soul. Over the years, having learned that harmonizing your soul is not the same thing as making it predictable, I've come to think that this is true. This being the rural South, where people seek all sorts of paths to grace, I'm often asked to think about miracles. And what I think is that if the snake handlers, the layers of hands, and the speakers in tongues are right about anything, it's this: miracles always look funny at first. "Strange is normal, normal is strange," I've taken to saying about the shop. It's the strange ones— the calmly, peacefully strange ones—who have got the harmonized souls. They may not be beautiful or lovable or even very smart, but they have something to teach you just the same.

Will Cisco—aka Storyteller, from Toms River, New Jersey—might have been one of those souls. He hiked into our store in the early summer complaining of hurt knees. The hostel was full when he arrived, so we put him down at the cabin. He hung out there for a couple of weeks, but it didn't take him more than a few days to make an impression, to fit himself into the life of the shop.

Wet, I don't think Will weighed more than 145 pounds. I never saw him without his camouflage flat cap with a pencil sticking out of the brim, which accentuated his big ears and long nose. His demeanor, his boyish slenderness, and the short, black-as-coal beard neatly etched on his face made him look younger than his age, fifty-two. He had three talents—he was a handyman, a baker, and a talker—and he pursued them energetically. He was in motion all the time: going here, chattering there, fixing this or that. If his hands or feet weren't moving, his mouth was. He remains one of the most talkative persons that I have ever met, and he wasn't very good at resting his injured knees. When he did stand still, he could be found in a crowd of people spinning a tale of his adventures while living in Yosemite during the late seventies and early eighties.

There were two stories he told me the very day he arrived, and I heard them again, more than once, before he was gone. The first came from the summer of 1976, when he camped in Little Yosemite Valley near Half Dome and Nevada Falls.

"It was midsummer in seventy-six, and I had been in Yosemite for a little over two months already, trying to hike as many trails as I could before someone decided it was way past the two weeks you're allowed to stay. One evening I found myself sharing a camp, having coffee and a joint, with three fellows. Two of them were brothers, and the third was a lifelong friend. One brother got around to telling me that they had some LSD and that he was going to take some the next day and climb to the top of Half Dome and dance a jig on the edge of the cliff. I told him, 'I'm looking at a dead man,' and of course he just laughed at that. He said good-bye to me the next morning, saying he'd see me at dinnertime, and then he climbed Half Dome and danced right off the cliff, to his death. The other two came back without him.

"The ranger had to go out looking for the body, and he asked me if I could stick around the next day and keep an eye on the campground for him; he also asked if I would mind giving some friends of his their food drop, which was locked in his cabin. Next afternoon, the ranger's friends came looking for him, and they found me, so I took them up to his cabin, gave them their food supplies. And as I'm walking back to camp, a man comes racing up the trail. He's frantic. Wants to know where the ranger was. I told him he was out on a search-and-rescue and asked him what was wrong, at which point he told me his buddy had cut his kneecap off with a hatchet.

"I told him to get back to camp, that I would help them. I still hadn't gotten out of my head what I'd said to that dead kid a couple nights before: 'I'm talking to a dead man.' I was still replaying it over and over, thinking that my words had doomed him.

"So we go running for the campsite as fast as we can. When we get there, I see a dozen or so people around, just looking at the guy, not doing a damn thing, except holding a shirt over the wound to stem the bleeding. I pushed through the crowd to take a closer look at his leg. There's this chunk of bone stuck in this mess, this flap of flesh, that's hanging on by about a half-inch of skin. It looked like a half-moon and was about the size of my palm. He had almost amputated the entire kneecap of his left leg.

"I told some people to start boiling water, and I asked him how this had happened. He said he and his buddies had brought a bunch of bottles of Wild Turkey with them; he had been drinking, then he decided to chop some firewood. So, being fairly drunk at that point, he decided to hold the wood he was chopping with his knee, and cut right next to it with his hand hatchet. Missed the wood. Got his knee instead.

"I explained that he needed surgery immediately or he would probably lose the kneecap and that outside help was at least eight hours away, probably more. I told him he had two options. First option: I could clean and dress the wound and hope that later on they might be able to do something for him, with the understanding that he would probably lose the kneecap. The other option was for me to sew it back in place, hoping that this would preserve it, so a doctor could fix it properly later. He said: do whatever it takes. So I told his friends to hold him and pour another pint of Wild Turkey down him. While that was taking place, I grabbed this big fellow who was standing there, pulled him to the side, asked if he threw a good punch. He said that when he was in the service he was his unit's boxing champ. I told him that when I was ready, I would give him the nod, and at that point, he should knock out my patient.

"I was carrying a curved upholstery needle and some nylon thread for pack repairs. I washed my hands, then sterilized that needle, the thread, and my toothbrush—sterilized it with more whiskey. Then I gave the boxer the nod, and he hauled off with a roundhouse punch that knocked the guy right off the log and out like a light.

"The surgery goes like this. I take two more bottles of Turkey and start dumping it onto the knee, use my toothbrush to scrub around the wound. I know tendons are cut, but I don't know what goes with what. I try to match them up as best I can, studying the cuts one at a time. It was like working with a toothpick-size puzzle and then trying to stitch the toothpick together. After I finished with the tendons, I sewed the cap of the knee back on. It took fifty-six stitches. When I was done, I sat back on a rock. I could feel the adrenaline flushing through my body. And you know what I said? I said: 'I need a joint and a drink.' In the morning, the rangers arrived, shot the guy up with Demerol, put an inflatable splint on him, and hauled him out on a mule; he was high as a kite and laughing. That was the last I ever saw of him.

"Five, six months later, in early December, I'm working at the Awahnee Hotel in the park when a ranger calls the kitchen and asks to speak with me. He told me he was down at the south entrance, and four guys were entering the park and that they were looking for a guy named Will who fit my description. He wanted to know, did I have a beef with anyone? No I didn't, I said. Tell them where to find me.

"They showed up at the back door of the kitchen two hours later. As it turned out, it was the brother and some friends of the fellow I had done knee surgery on. They were in the park for ten days during school break. His brother said that he figured I would still be around after all this time and he wanted to show his appreciation for saving his knee. Turns out he sent them with two hundred dollars, a big bag of good weed, and a camera, to prove that they had found me. They had to bring back either the money and the weed, or a picture of me.

"I rearranged my schedule to play tour guide for their stay, and they wined and dined me well. They told me that when the brother reached the hospital and finally saw a doctor, the doctor wanted to know why the surgeon had used sewing thread on him. To which his reply was, the surgeon was some twenty-year-old kid who did that up on the trail. The doc told him it looked like a professional had worked on him, and ordered his family doc to wait at least two weeks to remove the stitches; he said he couldn't have done a better job himself. Let me tell you: that sure made my day, to hear what high praise the doc had for my work."

The other story Will told the day I met him was a parable about choosing to live or die. Maybe he saw a chance to relieve his soul of an unwanted weight; maybe this was just his opening act in every place he went to. Remembering Will, I see now that I never entirely believed, strictly speaking, anything he told me. But then, he was a storyteller, not a journalist. Demanding historical accuracy of him would have been missing the point; his stories had a kind of sideways wisdom in them, whether they were true or not.

I don't recall asking Will if he had ever attempted suicide, and I don't know how the subject ever came up, as we had known each other for only about fifteen minutes at that time.

"Winton, I like you. I got a good sense of people."

"I like you too, Will. You seem like a nice guy."

"You know where I was a year ago? I was sitting on top of a twelve-foot ladder in the woods near my home in Jersey with one end of a rope tied around my neck and the other end tied to a tree. I must've sat on that ladder for five, maybe eight minutes, trying to get the courage to jump off. You see, my wife and I had been married for over twenty-five years, and she wanted a divorce. She ran off with one of my best friends—but that's not what bothered me. He was a nice guy. Anyway, eventually I did get the courage. I jumped off. The ladder kicks out, I start the fall, the rope pulls tight. . . . And then the rope snapped, and I hit my face flat against the ground."

"Divine intervention, maybe," I said.

"Maybe. Not sure. I busted my nose pretty good. It was the stupidest thing I've ever done. But you know what I did next?"

"I give up. What?"

"I got up, dusted myself off, and decided to go for a walk. That's why I am here, standing in front of this counter."

I proposed a moral for the story: when you're at the end of your rope, you go for a hike, I told him.

"I suppose you're right," Will said. "It's funny, the sort of luck that keeps you holding on to life, you know. One day, I sew a man's knee on with an upholstery needle; the next day, I can't even tie a knot."

Will-the-surgeon is one story I'm not going to forget. He told it to me a few days before John, Jennifer's ex-boyfriend, killed himself.

I'm at the register with Buddy. We're watching Jen do her best to calm down a short, fat, angry woman, who came in a few minutes ago and has been stamping in tight circles with a waggling finger in the air, giving out her story in fragments slipped in between curses and pauses to yank her undersized polyester stretch pants up over her hips. Her makeup of purples and pinks makes her face look bigger, and her golden earrings are half as big around as dinner plates. She says her man ran out on her at Vogel State Park.

"I don't trust him. Oh, could you get me couple of those Snickers bars? And throw in a bag of M&M's with peanuts; oh, and I'll take this Diet Coke, too. I think he's left me. Lord God almighty. Heaven help that man if he left me."

"Why do you say that?" Jennifer asks with a curious lift of her brow and a half grin.

"I just don't trust him. Never really have. I know he has left me. I been waiting here for three hours. He said they would only be out hiking for two hours. I just don't trust him or his little demon son, who hates my guts. Would you mind calling Vogel State Park and have them check on campsite forty-three and make sure that my trailer is still there? I just know they left me."

"Certainly they just wouldn't have picked up everything and left you here. We could probably find you a ride to Vogel. It's only three miles down the hill," says Jennifer.

"You don't know him, sugar. I been married three times, and I know a thing or two about men. I don't need men no more anyways. Just give me a box of chocolate and some batteries. That's all the pleasure I need, honey."

"Really, wow, that's awesome, a box of chocolates, cool," says Jennifer, trying to hold back laughter.

"That's right. You got the number to Vogel? Who knows, they may be packing up all that crap he brought into this bug-infested forest right now. How do you stand it up here, girl?"

Jennifer happily agrees to make the phone call. While she's dialing, Billy, who's standing by the door, waves me over.

"Look at this guy about to cross the street."

"What in the hell does he have over his shoulder?"

"Careful with your words. To me it looks to be about a hundred pounds of wooden cross."

"No shit. Heaven help us, you're right. It's a cross."

The bearer of the cross is very tall, over six feet four, in his midtwenties, with long, curly, mocha-brown hair, and as skinny as a toothpick. He's wearing a pair of green boxer shorts, sandals, and no shirt. He has a small knapsack on his back and a yellow stuff sack dangling from the top of the cross. He looks on the verge of collapse when he walks into the parking lot, and the expression on his face is one of regret. The hand-built cross is made of two large pieces of landscape timber; fastened to the bottom, like the punch line of a bad joke, is a six-inch rubber wheel.

"You want to ask him, or should I?" says Billy.

"I don't think we have to ask what he's doing. By the expression on his face, I would bet a hundred dollars that he's done doing it."

Billy chuckles. "I think you're right."

"Hey, Crucifix, you made it! We were getting a little worried!" shouts an older man standing on the gravel pathway.

Crucifix gives an upward nod of his head and acknowledges the voice. He slowly walks over to the grass by the mailbox, rolls the heavy cross off his shoulder, and watches it crash to the ground. He stands there looking at it for a couple of moments and then tosses his pack beside the cross and kicks at the grass. Looking up, he flips the brown curls from his eyes, exposing a fuller view of a dirty, sharp-jawed face. He explores the landscape with his eyes, looking left, right, up, and finally turning around, as if he's looking for an escape route. He leans down, reaches into his pack, and pulls out his water bottle, which is empty, and walks toward the stairs.

"Well, Billy, he's headed our way. Now's your chance to get his story for that little journal of yours."

"I know that story," Billy says. "Heard it a million times."

Before I can respond, Will walks up, with his mouth going a mile a minute. "Excuse me? I don't mean to interrupt, Winton, but you got a lot more plumbing problems down there in that rental cabin than just a leaky toilet. Whoever built that thing put quarter-inch piping in there, when they should've used half-inch. And whoever redid that bathroom floor didn't do you any favors. Some of the plywood isn't even sitting on the joist. If you try to put tile in there, the whole thing's just going crack up in a month. Now, my knee's pretty jacked up right now, and I could use another week off of it. If you're willing to give me a place to stay and maybe trade me some gear, I can fix most of that stuff. I don't need much."

The cabin is about two miles from the store, near Helton Creek Falls. Margie and I bought it just a few months earlier, as an investment. But it is also a place to put up hikers during the busy months, when the hostel overflows. We knew it was a fixer-upper, though we didn't have a lot of time or money to put into it. But there were always amateur tradesmen like Will coming off the Trail, ready to barter their skills for a meal and a place to sleep. More than one of my home-improvement projects have been solved this way.

I tell Will we'll work something out. "Just get me a list of everything you need, tell me how long you think it will take, and we'll go from there."

And that's when it's Alpine's turn to rush up behind me and take me by the shoulder. "Winton. You're not going to believe this." There's not a trace of his usual humor or spirit in his eyes.

Jennifer walks past us, out to the parking lot, and stands there alone and very still.

"Try me," I say.

"John did it. The dude killed himself."

The night after Alpine placed us in lockdown, Jennifer did break up with John, and, as predicted, he didn't take the news well. John fumed for three days, trying to get Jennifer to reconsider and begging her to meet with him. She smartly refused, and eventually she stopped answering his phone calls, which were becoming more frequent and aggressive every day. Jennifer regretted having to shut John out of her life. The love she'd had for him was gone, but she had mourned its loss like a friend's passing. Out of respect for the memory of their good days, she wished she could console him, lend him an ear, and she knew that no one else would. Jennifer loved everybody, found the good and the beauty in everything. She charmed those around her into revealing their hidden talent, their secret value, their best self, just by believing that it was there. This was her magic.

I don't know if Jennifer lost some of her magic that day, or traded it for wisdom, but I do know that she changed a little, became a shade more solemn.

A week before he died, John had entered the restaurant where Jennifer worked her second job. He grew impatient and surly when she asked another waitress to take his table. John insisted that Jennifer serve him, and made several belligerent comments, before he proclaimed to Jennifer and the entire restaurant that he was going to kill himself on her birthday, so she would never forget him, and stormed out. He left no note and died, of a drug overdose, three days before Jennifer's birthday. It was ruled an accidental death. He may not have known what day it was.

I really don't understand death, but it seems to be a popular pastime, considering the fact that more than one hundred fifty thousand people per day participate worldwide. I wonder: in all that number, how many are not so different in life from John? He wasn't a horrible man—just a little misguided, a little misunderstood, probably a little overlooked. He didn't have the right equipment was what I found myself sadly thinking, with my outfitter's brain, when I remembered John and the dusty old tool belt that he wore. Of those one hundred fifty thousand, how many are likewise underequipped? What's the equipment that we need most of all?

The answer may be a kind of eagerness to celebrate everyday blessings, a grateful love of life's small joys and gifts. Look up, smile, and dance. I think I heard the voice of the Wind Walkers once. I hope I don't forget it; I hope it speaks to others.

My patience with the human species, though it gets me into trouble now and then, is something I take pride in. I do have a threshold, where my patience ends—where, as Margie says, I have to "hit the reset button." But that point seems to be higher than most people's. It took years to develop patience, and I have not mastered the task, but I'm committed to the effort. Patience fosters peace of mind, of course, but it's also singularly useful in my line of work. After all, to work for dedicated hikers is to serve people who are driven by obsessions: living in the woods is a crazy act, and it requires a crazy motive. Having the ability to accept the fact that people are different, that each will follow his own path in life; having the humility not to pretend to know, or need to know, why people move as they do; having the patience to hear out each crazy motive for each crazy act—this is how to earn the trust of a wandering soul. Patience is the key that unlocks understanding.

Will required some patience, but he never pushed me too close to my threshold. I marveled at his stories—not that they were so different from backwoods stories I'd heard before, but that there were so many of them, that he was so full of them. He could line up one story after another, burning them down like cigarettes, all night long. There was always another story. Whether he had an extraordinary memory or he was an extraordinary liar, he intrigued me either way. He seemed to annoy the hell out of everyone else.

Once I gave the approval on the materials to fix the unstable floor and the leaking pipes in the old red cabin, Will went right to work. He stayed down at the cabin most of the day and would labor tirelessly. He was a perfectionist, and every day he would add something to his list: leaky faucet, creaky doorjamb, stuck window, wobbly ceiling fan. And he turned the cabin into his private bakery. It seemed he always had something in the oven for staff, desserts mostly—cookies, brownies, or cupcakes. At first the staff resisted his gifts, for fear that he had laced them with some mind-altering drug that he was not revealing. After the first week, once a few brave eaters had spread the word that Will's brownies were tasty and, unless he specifically noted otherwise, nonnarcotic, it appeared that Will was building some friendships with the staff and that they were becoming more comfortable with him. But then he would do or say something that made them dubious again.

A good example occurred during the day we learned of John's death. Will was at the computer in the back of the shop after we had gotten the news.

"Winton, Nate!" he shouted. "I think I have a date!"

"A date?" I said. "Hell, you only been here—what? A week? And who do you know here, in the middle of nowhere?"

"Yeah, yeah. I meet them on Friday."

"Them? You meet them?" Nate said.

"Yeah, isn't this great?" Will said. "Found them on swingers-dot-com. They live down in Cleveland. What's that—about fifteen, twenty miles away?"

Nate and I stepped in toward the computer. Nate, the practical man, wanted to know the details. "So, do they, like, send you pictures?" he asked, as he inched a little closer to the screen.

"Of course. We've been talking back and forth for a few days. They seem like a nice couple."

"How long have you been . . . swinging?" Nate asked.

"Well, it's been for—"

Felicity interrupted. "Winton, this guy up front wants to speak to a manager."

The guy up front was a heavyset twenty-year-old kid who said he'd bought forty-five dollars' worth of food the day before. A bear had stolen the food in the night. The kid figured we ought to replace it.

That's the sort of thing that makes me reach for the reset button.

I informed the kid that, like it or not, he'd bought a forty-five-dollar dinner for a bear, and I told him where he could find the hostel's hiker box, where people leave food behind.

"I'll be back!" he whined as he went out. "This isn't over!"

"What's with these kids?" said Buddy, who had witnessed our exchange. "If I acted like that when I was a kid, my daddy would have knocked me out. You have more patience than me. A lot more patience than me."

Outside on the balcony, at the end of that long day, friends gather over a cooler of beer. There are two kinds of beer, for two beer-drinking philosophies. There are bottles of Yuengling, brought by Nate, and there are cans of Natural Light, from Pirate. Half of us think Natural Light is about as good as drinking watery piss, and the other half thinks Yuengling costs too much. Teasing each other's taste becomes a safe harbor for conversation, a place to drift back to when there is nothing else to say.

Nate has brought out his guitar, and Alpine is setting up his bongos. Pirate leans against the wall, holding a can of Natural Light while posing for pictures being taken by a woman in a purple paisley sundress. Billy is sitting on the picnic table trying to tune his flute while Margie and Felicity dig through the cooler looking for Yuenglings, exchanging jibes with the canned-beer drinkers. A dozen or more hikers stand to the side along the walkway, watching the staff and their various instruments assembling on the balcony—curious, as people are, to see what the shopkeepers do when they close up at day's end. Will has trapped an audience of three hikers against the south wall, and he's regaling them with one of his Yosemite tales. I call over with a smile: "Hey, Will, tell me about that 'them' date you have on Friday."

"Oh yeah, I'll be right there," he says, and excuses himself from the hikers. "I'll be right back. Don't go away, guys. You gotta hear the part about the plane crash and the bales of frozen weed in the lake."

Buddy grabs a can out of Pirate's cooler, and I head for the Yuengling. Will comes over to the table, and appears to forget his reason for coming. He stands before us swaying, soaked in good vibes, grinning sweetly: stoned.

"Eh, Will," I say, "anybody ever told you that you look like that guy Jeebs in the *Men in Black* movie? You know, the guy that Tommy Lee Jones kept blowing his head off, and the damn thing would just grow right back?"

Will retorts, "I remember Jeebs. He's the one who had that deneuralyzer thingy that they needed in order to get Tommy Lee Jones's character's memory back. No, man. I like that dude."

"Yeah, and if you keep smoking whatever you're smoking, you may need a deneuralyzer to get your memory back," Buddy says with a chuckle. "Don't you know that boys from Toms River, Jersey, are already born with half a brain? You better stop wasting it."

"Buddy, settle. Old Will has reason to celebrate. He has a date on Friday. He's meeting them in Cleveland."

"Them? A double date?" asks Buddy.

"No," says Will, "it's just three of us."

It's the first time ever, I have to believe, that Buddy has been at a complete loss for words.

Over the next thirty minutes we learn about the life and the justification of a swinger. Will and his wife swung together for twenty-plus years; the "nice guy" she ran off with was one of their swinging partners. This was a painful test of his principles, but in the end Will came through, and he says the divorce didn't change his thinking. The fact is, he says, mammals are not monogamous by nature. "Monogamy is rare in the whole animal kingdom. Less than four percent of mammals are known to have one lifelong mate: beavers, otters, foxes, and, strangely, jackals are monogamous. Yet sometimes they all stray."

"Penguins, right?"

"Yes, penguins too. But I was talking about mammals, man."

Will explains that if more people were like him, their relationships and marriages would be stronger, happier—more biologically honest, therefore more spiritually fulfilling. "You see, I loved my wife—I still love my wife—and we were happy for many, many years. We were free of jealousy, which made us freer in marriage. Although we're separated, we're still friends. We understood early in our relationship that monogamy was the oddity in nature, not promiscuity, and that is why we stayed together for so long."

I'm feeling the tickle of a thought which doesn't allow itself to be grasped until later, when I catch Margie from the right angle at sunset, and the thought makes itself clear: Isn't that what's magnificent about lifelong love? That it's unnatural—that it's better than nature?

In my frame of reference, there's not much room for Will's logic, but it's not my place to judge him. To me, swinging sounds like an unfortunate cross between sex and pickup basketball—but Will's account of himself, won from twenty years of experience, is no less interesting for that. It is the differences in people—Will, Minnesota Smith, the Samsonite Twins, Nimblewill Nomad, Preacher Man, even Lefty—that make this place what it is. Maybe if we all celebrated these differences more, we would see our commonalities better.

Buddy, still standing next to me, has rolled his eyes during the conversation so many times, I think they've come loose in their sockets. Finally Will decides he's thirsty and reaches for one of Pirate's Natural Lights, cracks open the tab, and takes a sip, allowing me to interject and change topics.

I ask Buddy what happened with the woman who came in this morning. "Did the husband and son take off on her?"

"No, they finally showed up. Three hours late. That woman was a piece of work. She wouldn't shut up. I think she bought every romance paperback novel from our used-book section and nearly wiped me out of hot dogs on the spinner rack. Will, I don't even like you that much, and I wouldn't have set you up with that lady. She blessed me so many times you'd think I was a prophet. Lord help the idiot that's married that woman."

"Buddy, do you find the good in anything?" Will asks.

"Yeah, I saw good and greatness when the damn husband showed up. Speaking of that, I gotta go let Damn Dog out at the house before he pisses all over everything. See you in the morning."

"Damn Dog?" someone says. "Is that its name?"

"I thought it was named after a cartoon, Buddy."

"Yeah," Buddy says. "Its name is Brutus."

The hikers soon felt comfortable enough to join us on the balcony, and before the night was over, a few more coolers appeared along the stone wall from places unknown. Nate was picking a few soft chords on his guitar, and Alpine was trying to match his rhythm with the bongos; Jennifer sat behind Alpine, her arms around his shoulders. As always, Billy fussed and fiddled with his Coyote Oldman flute but never raised it to his lips; he just gently stroked it and fingered its stops, as if he would have it play spontaneous, magical music or no music at all.

At some point, we all observed a moment of silence for John: the staff, the hikers who had joined us, the strangers from the hostel, people who had never known him, or never known him well—we all alike raised our bottles and cans. I think this was enough. A smaller gesture would have been inadequate, a grander one insincere. We let our fellowship serve respect to John's memory. For most of us, he had been a stranger who had not found comfort and shelter when he needed it. So Mountain Crossings would go on providing comfort and shelter.

Through the night, Pirate leaned on the wall, keeping two beers in his hand and two more buried in the front pocket of his nylon pants. He didn't do that because he was a drunk, but because he was gracious. The extra beers in his pocket were for people he liked; the two in his hands were his.

I asked him if he'd seen the guy with the cross.

"Crucifix. Yep. Talked to 'im."

"What happened to him?"

"He left."

"Headed up the Trail?"

"Nope. Headed up the yellow-blaze towards Blairsville. Want a beer?"

"Thanks. Did he have that cross with him?"

"Nope. That's still layin' over there in the grass by the mailbox. I suppose he had a new revelation." Pirate winked.

"What did he say to you?"

"Said he found Jesus up on Blood Mountain, and said Jesus talked to him, and that Jesus ain't ever talked to him before. He said Jesus walked with him too."

"What did Jesus say?"

"I guess He told him to get the hell off this mountain."

Alpine and Jennifer take in the trail.

CHAPTER NINETEEN
International Man of Mystery

My printer is an old dot-matrix. I keep it because it's cheap to run, and I like the singing clatter it makes as it pounds the letters across the page, like some cross between an old typewriter and an electric saw. I rip the strange e-mail—full of typos and bad punctuation—from the rollers and head toward the balcony, where Alpine is trying to convince some twenty-year-old kid that he doesn't need to carry a full-length hatchet and a two-foot bow saw. The kid is starting to get irritated—he loves his hardware.

"Okay, let's say you need one of 'em. You don't need both. Why don't you give up the bow saw and maybe cut half the handle off that hatchet?"

"No way, dude. I like the feel of a full-length hatchet in my hand."

"Winton, would you tell him?"

I tell him: "Friend, there are two things that a hatchet like that is good at doing in these woods: freaking the shit out of every hiker and little boy you camp with over the next few months, and carving a gash into your leg so large that you'll wish you had brought a gun so you could shoot yourself in the head."

"We know a guy who knew a guy," Alpine says, "who cut his damn kneecap off with a hatchet."

"Cut his kneecap off?" The kid is frozen in horror.

"*Ffffffffft*," Alpine says, swiping his hand through the air. "Imagine that."

I ask Alpine for a word in private. We leave the kid on the balcony—holding his saw and his hatchet, staring at his knees—and walk up to the higher overlook, a small clearing about fifty yards up the hill behind the store. Alpine rests his foot on the stone that bears a plaque commemorating W. R. Neel, the surveyor of the American Scenic Highway that around 1920 would be laid through what was then known as Frogtown Gap.

I hand Alpine the printout. "This just came in. Something about a relative in an accident in Norway. Sounds like a can of crap to me."

Alpine throws a casual glance at the page, with a chuckle and a smirk, but then his face turns ghostlike, and his eyes seem to drop into some inward abyss. He takes a half step back, as though he needs the extra space to gather his thoughts.

"What's wrong? Is it real? Do you know this 'Patrick' fellow?"

Swallowing, he says: "No. It's probably my ex-father-in-law, Max. He gave me and Mariek some money when we got married, and now that we're divorced, he wants me to pay him back. How did he find you?"

"That's not hard. I'm running a business, Alpine. I'm trying to be found. And pictures of you are all over my Web site. What do you want me to tell him?"

"Tell him you haven't seen me."

"Fine with me." Assuming that Alpine is correct, and that this "Patrick" is really Max, I decide to stay out of the whole situation for the moment and respond to "Patrick."

PATRICK—thanks for the e-mail. Haven't seen James in while. . . sorry I couldn't help. Regards

—WINTON

Alpine had it all. It only made sense that others would want a piece.

All of us at the shop had heard about the two condominiums in Miami, the plans to develop a resort on the three acres in Hawaii, the monthly military retirement check, the trust fund full of cash that included the land in Norway that Alpine leased to a local farmer for grazing livestock. If we sometimes measured our lives against Alpine's—if now and then, pouring antifreeze into a toilet on a cold morning, I saw myself in one of those Miami condos—our envy never lasted long against our love for him. What stood out about Alpine, far more than his wealth, were his loose, easy style, his simple tastes, and his unhesitating loyalty to his friends. This was not a man who rubbed his success in your face, or who used his money to draw boundaries around himself. And he had been a soldier, an adventurer, a wise investor; how could you hold his money against him? We were proud of him, and he made us proud of ourselves. He was handsome, wealthy, rugged, had been all over the world, and he claimed to love no place better than our Mountain Crossings. He could go anywhere, and he stayed with us. He made us all feel a little more glamorous.

Until a few days later, when two more strange e-mails showed up in my box, and Alpine's glamour started to flake off, like shiny paint.

To: Mr Winton Porter
FROM: Carlos Puchades

Hello I am Carlos Puchades from newportrichey fl, I am trying to plan a hiking trip for my family.
I would like to get some info on some of your best and most experienced staff with pictures. and a history of them selfs.

THANKYOU.

HI WINTONY

Just been looking what's on offer on your website, saw your picture gallery and . . . . surprise surprise there are some piccies from my old mate Jimmy , is he in your employ ? can you kindly ask him to contact me and/or where can I get hold of him.

REGARDS
BRIAN WHITE
Currently in the Ardennes — Belgium

Mountain Crossings has never led or guided trips on the Appalachian Trail, but it's commonly assumed that we do. So Carlos's first request is not that unusual; his interest in pictures of my staff and "a history of them selfs," however, is very unusual. The second e-mail from Mr. White about his "surprise, surprise" finding of "piccies" of his "old mate Jimmy," with its forced informality and its made-up slang, is just bizarre. My instinct is starting to stir questions in my mind.

Again I print the e-mails and go in search of Alpine. This time I find him in the parking lot, loading a stack of large blue Tupperware containers into the back of his Isuzu Rodeo. A surfboard and two bikes lean against the back bumper.

I shove the e-mails into my pocket and stop halfway down the stairs to study the scene for a moment. He tries shoving the containers in; they don't fit; he tosses some bundles and bags around and smacks the Tupperware into place. He's frustrated, and he's trying to control any outward appearance of panic. I get within two steps of him without his noticing. His focus is limited to only what is a few feet in front of him.

"Where you going?"

"Huh? Ah, what?"

"Where are you headed?"

"I'm picking some stuff up that I had in the shed, and I am outta here," he says angrily, eyes narrowed. "People around here don't give me the respect that I deserve."

Alpine digs into his pocket, then holds out his hand, exposing a small green-and-blue patch in the shape of a shield divided by a cross: embroidered in the top left corner is the sun, and in the lower right corner, a star; a diagonal red lightning bolt separates the two down the middle of the patch. He has shown it to me before. It's the patch of the 75th Ranger Regiment. Alpine slams it on top of one of the blue bins in front of him.

"I earned this patch. I went willing and proudly out there to lay my life on the line for these kids, and none of them give a damn. In the Army, if any of these kids disrespected me like they do around here, I would've had them shoveling shit out of latrines for a week."

Out where? To which honorable military engagement? What kids? Disrespecting him how? The hard-bitten veteran routine doesn't sound like Alpine—the complaint is too vague, too generic, too Hollywood. It's a disguise.

"Civilian life is different. I don't blame you for wanting to pack everything up and head somewhere else. Some days, I wish I could do the same thing. Let me help you get some of this loaded," I say as I grab a bin.

"I just don't get it," Alpine rants, punching some cargo around. "I have spent my entire life in and around the military. My father was a colonel. My sister is a senior master sergeant in the Air Force. It's the only thing in life I know. I love this place. It's the only place where I have ever felt like I was at home. But I just can't stay. I need to go where my skills are appreciated, respected."

"What about Jennifer?"

His shoulders relax and his tone softens. "She's coming with me. We're going to Colorado. I have a friend who owns an adventure-travel company, and he needs some help. We've been talking about it a lot."

"Where is she?"

"She's mountain-biking with her brother Danny." Pause.

"Is this really what's bothering you?"

He just looks at me. Whatever is bothering him isn't about "these kids" not showing respect. Nor is he simply pursuing a better life. He's running, and the only clues I have as to why now sit in my back pocket, on the pages of those e-mails. Who is Alpine, really? Why do these people want to find him? What has he done?

Felicity calls from the top of the stairs, saying they need some help in the store. I tell Alpine to say good-bye before he goes. After helping Felicity, Nate, and Buddy with the normal weekend crowd lined up for sodas, candy bars, trail advice, and minor pack repairs, I return to my computer. There is already another e-mail on the screen, obviously linking back to the previous ones; only this time the return address does reveal someone named "Max." So Alpine was right about that.

> **DEAR WINTON**
>
> Just a short "Thank You" for covering-up for Jimmy the boy is now useless and doesn't know what's going to hit him next ! and there is no doubt that you will be held responsible for 'hiding' this Boy disrupting the cause of justice!!!!
>
> Mr Hess has been fully briefed on your behaviour backing-up this WANTED criminal !
>
> Good riddance.
>
> **FATHER OF No= 3 WIFE OF JIMMY**

I read the cryptic e-mail three more times, the phrases striking like terrible bells. *Wanted criminal. Number-three wife. The cause of justice, covering up, hiding, disrupting. Held responsible.*

What in the hell has Alpine—aka Jimmy (though rarely around here)—done? He is starting to sound like the evil twin to the man I thought I knew.

I go back outside. The Rodeo is still in the parking lot, but there is no sign of Jimmy. I see Jennifer and her brother Danny unloading their bicycles from the back of Danny's truck. I come down the steps, and she crosses the lot to meet me. Danny gives me a serious look over his shoulder, then turns back around to fake some business with the bikes. He fiddles with the brake levers and tries to eavesdrop. Jennifer meets me in the middle of the lot.

"Winton, we need to talk," she says.

"I know we need to talk. Alpine says you're moving to Colorado. I suppose I should congrat—"

"No, we need to talk. Did you know he's still married to his wife in Miami? That he has been married three times? Did you know that he has a sixteen-year-old son in Pennsylvania and a twelve-year-old daughter in Norway? Did you know this?"

"No, I didn't know this. How do you know this?"

"Danny told me that Alpine's father-in-law found my father and talked to him. Danny wasn't supposed to say anything, but when he saw Alpine packing everything up, Danny decided that I needed to know."

"Where is Alpine now?"

"He's next door. Packing his shit up." Giving in to anger, she spits out the words, raking her fingers through her hair. "What should I do?"

I tell her that I am no psychologist and that we need more information.

"I don't even know who this man is." Jennifer starts to cry. "He proposed to me."

Well, it's your choice, I think. Walk away, or go introduce yourself.

Danny comes over and lays his hand on his sister's shoulder. She cries softly while he provides me with details of their family's conversation with the father-in-law, Max. Apparently, Max hired a private investigator to help find Sergeant James-Jimmy-Alpine Ingram. Warrants for Ingram's arrest were uncovered somewhere in Pennsylvania, for back child support owed to his first wife and her son—Ingram's first child, a boy who is now sixteen. From there the trail led to a second wife in Norway and Ingram's second child, a girl, age twelve. The third, and allegedly the current, wife, Mariek, lives in Miami and is the daughter of the pissed-off Max. I'm not sure how Mariek and Ingram met, but it seems that she went for him because he was an American who could speak Norwegian.

Meanwhile, Max, scheming his revenge in Norway, is trying to figure out how to apprehend Ingram before he escapes the mountains of North Georgia and have him extradited to Pennsylvania. That's why he swore Jennifer's family to secrecy for a few days while he masterminded the arrest with his high-priced PI, Mr. Hess—the same Mr. Hess who has been "fully briefed" on my "behaviour."

I ask Danny if we are supposed to expect another convoy of FBI agents up the mountain.

"I don't know. This is some crazy stuff."

Welcome to my world, Danny. We specialize in crazy.

Jennifer and Danny leave to find Alpine and talk to him, at my advice. "See if you can get the other side of the story," I say. "That's the least we can do." I stay at the shop, where tense gossip is already buzzing. Two hours pass, as slow and heavy as a hike up Blood Mountain in a cold rainstorm. We monitor the parking lot, expecting a caravan of police and wondering what we'd say to them. I check my e-mail for another crazed note from Brian of Belgium or Carlos of "newportrichey" or Mad Max (aka Patrick) of Norway. It isn't until I have locked up the shop that Alpine finally appears. He looks like a man who has just spent half the day in a confessional booth: eyes swollen, face sullen.

Honesty and other virtues are like muscles: you have to keep them in shape. James Ingram's honesty has just gotten more exercise than it has had in years, and he is exhausted. It is easy to sense that he doesn't want to go another round with me. He leans against his truck and folds his arms, waiting for me at the bottom of the stairs. I am not in a kindly mood when I get there.

"Well, you look like crap," I say. "I suspect that a lot of what I have learned today is true, and you don't need to explain yourself to me right now. At this point, I just want to know three things. Are you still married? Are there any dead bodies involved? And should we expect the police?"

"Yes, I am still legally married to Mariek. No dead bodies. And it is unlikely the police will arrest me here in Georgia for a missed-child-support warrant." Here Alpine at last meets my eye, and he gives just the slightest bitter smile. "That, I knew nothing about."

I tell him to get some rest and we'll deal with this later, that I'm not going to kick him out of my life.

I didn't see Alpine or Jennifer for the next two days. During that time, Alpine dominated our conversations in the store, and within a day the story had found its way up the Appalachian Corridor and onto nearly every Trail forum. He had already been a part of the fabric of the Trail, but now he was getting a much larger square on the quilt. Alpine was becoming an unwilling Trail legend.

I received two more e-mails from Max over the next few days. One was an invitation to his Facebook page to view his photo album, which I never did. The next one simply read:

"GOOD JOB! LOCK 'M UP"

It takes four days before Alpine agrees to sit down with me and tell his side of the story. He's not eager to face me, and he's still trying to salvage a relationship with Jennifer that he fears he has blistered beyond healing. We meet at the store after everyone is gone. The store is closed.

The "debriefing" of Master Sergeant James Ingram goes something like this:

Winton Porter: Want a beer? I got a few hidden in the cooler.

Sergeant James Ingram: No, thanks.

Porter: Well, hope you don't mind if I have one. (Smiling.) Wish you had brought some popcorn.

Sergeant Ingram: We can go and get some.

Porter: Listen, you know you don't owe me an explanation. It's your life, and you can carry on with it without ever having to tell me anything.

Sergeant Ingram: I want to. This place means a lot to me. Jennifer means a lot to me. You guys are the only real family that I ever had outside of the military. I never knew why I ended up here exactly, and I didn't know why I kept coming back, until now."

Porter: Well, let's start from the beginning. My name is Winton Porter. What is yours, again?

Sergeant Ingram: It's Master Sergeant James Ingram.

Porter: Master sergeant. So the part about your military background is true.

Sergeant Ingram: Yes, sir. That part is true.

Porter: What about the property in Hawaii? The two condos in Miami? Land and trust funds in Norway?

Sergeant Ingram: I had a small trust fund set up after my father died. I spent most of that money traveling, hiking, and climbing, in the United States and Europe mostly. I don't own three acres in Hawaii, and the condo in Miami, Mariek owns. The second condo I told you that I bought last year along Miami Beach was made up. I have a lot of family in Norway, because that's where my mother's from, but I don't have land there.

Porter: What about your mom? Is she dead or alive?

Sergeant Ingram: She's alive. She divorced my dad several years before he died. She ran off with another woman. I never could fully accept that part of her life, and we haven't spoken in years.

Porter: What about your kids?

Sergeant Ingram: It's true I have two kids. A boy in Pennsylvania and a daughter in Norway.

His story plays out this way: He met his first wife in Pennsylvania when he was on leave from Fort Benning, near Columbus in east central Georgia, in 1991: "I was only nineteen, young and dumb. She was twenty-one. Beautiful, and tons of fun," he says. The fun soon led to pregnancy, and Ingram did the honorable thing and married wife number one. They moved to Fort Benning, where Ingram was training, and the marriage was on the rocks from the beginning. Ingram headed off to another tour in Kuwait, and when he came back, his checking accounts were empty, and his wife was gone. She went back home to Pennsylvania, and they both filed for a divorce. The settlement required Ingram to pay child support, but he didn't. His reasoning was, he says, "I didn't know if I was going to be dead next week or next month, and she didn't want me in her life or the kid's life, so I just never paid." He also says that he didn't know about the arrest warrant in Pennsylvania, but that he called the desk officer yesterday and was told that if he sent three thousand dollars, the authorities would lift the warrant and work out a payment plan.

Sergeant Ingram: I can get the money. And they have already intercepted my tax returns, and as of yesterday, they will start garnishing my monthly military retirement checks, but that's okay. I'll take responsibility. And if I work hard, maybe I can pay it off quickly. I want to help him.

Porter: What about the daughter in Norway?

Sergeant Ingram: It's less complicated. I haven't seen her since she was about eight months old, but I did ask a friend to go check on her about six years ago and make sure she was all right. Nikolina is twelve now and has a brother and sister. I doubt she even knows that I exist. The family pretty much asked me to leave.

My second wife—I met her when I was twenty-three and stationed in Hawaii. We spent two weeks together, partying, dancing—you know, having fun. We met again a few months later in Washington, DC, before she headed home to Norway. I had some time on my hands, family in Norway, so I followed her to Norway. She was gorgeous, funny, liked to hike, and she was always the life of the party. We partied nearly every night in the coffeehouses and bars in Norway. It was a lot of fun. She was a lot of fun. One thing led to another, and she ended up pregnant.

Things changed quickly. She went from short skirts to long dresses, church twice a week—Pentecostal, the Evangelical Lutherans, and so on. The religion just didn't make sense to me. I wouldn't go to church, and that didn't sit well with the family. The rules were strict in the township where we lived. They ticketed me twice for washing my car on Sunday. I didn't fit into their society or the family, so they asked me to leave. I didn't want to leave my daughter, but it was for the best.

I was still young. So I crawled back into my uniform and went off to do what I was trained to do, again not knowing if I would be dead next week or next month.

The years pass, 9/11 happens, and now I find myself leading a team of men through the mountains in Afghanistan. Within a year, I'm crawling out of a downed helicopter that had taken enemy fire and crashed, while trying to return fire on a bunch of rags who believe that they get twelve virgins in heaven when they die and watching two of my brothers die beside me. Life is crazy.

Porter: Do you think about her?

Sergeant Ingram: All the time. I think about both of them all the time. You don't know what a relief it is to get this off my shoulders. It's liberating. (Smiles.)

Porter: What about Mariek?

Sergeant Ingram: I tried to get back together with her when I left here the first time, but we have nothing in common, really. She was a good person and I liked her, all in all, but we were complete opposites. She liked walking in malls, and I liked hiking in the woods.

Porter: What about Mad Max?

Sergeant Ingram: He's just pissed off, and I really can't blame him. His little girl got shaded, and he wants revenge. I would have probably done the same thing.

Porter: Will he be coming after us?

Sergeant Ingram: I don't think so. I asked Mariek to call off the old dog. There's really nothing he can do. He doesn't understand the laws in the U.S., and when he uncovered a warrant for my arrest, he thought for certain that I was going to jail. But that's not the way it works on something like child support. Plus, I want to pay. I will pay this off.

Porter: Where did Mariek think you were, until her father tracked you down here?

Sergeant Ingram: Training a sled-dog team in Alaska.

Porter: How am I supposed to believe anything you say?

Sergeant Ingram: I don't know. I'm just glad that the truth is coming out.

(The conversation goes on long into the night. . . .)

Porter: So go get some sleep and be back at work at 8:30 in the morning. Got it?

Sergeant Ingram: Roger that!

Porter: And go see a doctor about the lying crap. It's not something that you can turn off overnight, you know.

Sergeant Ingram: Yes, sir.

Looks like Demetri "Coup" Coupounas, the founder and head of the GoLite company, has a little trouble downsizing some gear.

CHAPTER TWENTY
Living in the
Breezeway of Life

If places have souls, then the soul of Mountain Crossings is its covered breezeway. It is here, along the seven paces of the Appalachian Trail that pass under my roof and between my house and my store, that Mountain Crossings earns the right to its name. This is the crossing itself, the place of passage, the scene of transformation. Here, those who come in weary and doubtful may go out with fresh determination; those who come in dismayed after the thirty hard miles from where the trail begins, at Springer Mountain, may go out delighted to welcome more than two thousand more; here, wanderers become friends, and friends become wanderers again.

Like them, the precious things in life are changing all the time. Sierra's eyes have begun to take on the playfully wise look of her mother's; Allison is getting Margie's wild, quick smile; and when I sit and dream in the breezeway, my heart fills with what I suppose I should call a prayer. Let me be a grateful man.

"Sierra, move in a little closer to your daddy—you're covering up the white blaze on the wall. Allison, can you hold your new puppy up a little higher? Sky, look at me. Margie, don't move. You look perfect, wonderful, adorable; love that smile."

"Billy, are you taking a picture or trying to score a date with my wife?"

"Sensitive, aren't we? Okay, everybody say 'Walasi-Yi!' "

"Are we done now, Billy?" Allison asks. "Patches is a little hard to hold. She's a squirmy puppy."

"Not yet. Alpine and Jennifer, you're next. Stand over there in the breezeway. After this, I want a picture of everybody. Someone go find Pirate. And didn't I see Baltimore Jack walk in today? Sierra, would you go find Jack?"

It's picture day for Billy, which tells me that he's leaving on an extended journey soon. Yesterday, when I saw his old pack propped by the hostel door, I asked him where, and he said he wasn't really sure.

"Thought that I would head west for a little while and hike in Yosemite. I haven't been there in a few years, and I got an old friend out there I haven't seen in a while. You want to come?"

"I always want to come. Maybe next time."

"That's what you said last year."

"When are you headed out?" I asked him, knowing he wouldn't say. He smiled, whistled Sky over, and rubbed her behind the ears.

It could be today or tomorrow, but it will be within a week. The winds will know.

Meanwhile, our parade of characters continues. The heaviest pack ever carried into Mountain Crossings came in on top of a staggering, cursing, wretched Demetri "Coup" Coupounas. Billy and I were standing near the breezeway, discussing his plans for departure, when Coup came down the Trail from Blood Mountain.

"Good God," Billy said and pointed across the road. A group of hikers gathered, and we watched Coup's painful-looking last fifty yards.

"What is that?"

"Does he have a piano in there?"

"Maybe it's Santa Claus."

"I can't tell if the pack's carrying the man or the man's carrying the pack."

"Looks like an ant bringing home dinner."

When he crossed the road, shouting (over the screeching brakes of a car that almost ran him over on the curve) into a cell phone, I recognized him.

"That's Coup," I said. "He ain't dead after all."

Billy said he looked like he was pretty close.

We'd had word that Coup was out there attempting to break a hiking record of 620 miles in forty days, but that was more than a week ago; we had assumed that he had vanished from the Trail or had never been on it in the first place.

Coup is a loud talker, and by the time he'd managed to wrestle his pack off and stiffly return a wave of greeting, we had caught the drift of his cell phone conversation. After 30 tough-as-nails miles from the southern start, he was giving up on the other 590.

"Yeah. Pick me up at Neels Gap. What time do you think? Ten o'clock. Fine. Hold on. I'm getting another call. Hello? Yeah, I'm just getting a ride now. See if you can find me a flight out first thing tomorrow morning. I'll call you back when I'm on the road. Okay, bye. Hello? Yeah, ten o'clock, we said. Tonight, then. Okay. Okay. Bye."

The first and the last time I'd seen Coup had been at a convention of outdoor retailers in Salt Lake City, five years ago. He had made a powerful but not very agreeable impression on me at the time. Then he was a brash, bustling entrepreneur whose fledgling Colorado company was heading into its second year of business; his company had some new ideas, and Coup was scrapping and shoving and hobnobbing to get those ideas out there, on the map. He may not have had time for a sense of humor. I remembered him as a short, muscular, phenomenally stressed-out guy, a cannonball of entrepreneurial passion who was just a little too much to handle.

Now I watched him shuffle slowly along the gravel pathway toward the breezeway, dragging a backpack stuffed to the size of a washing machine.

He came up to me with a huge grin, followed by loud laughter: "I think that this is the dumbest fucking thing I've ever tried to do," Coup said.

"How much did you start with?" I asked.

"Hundred and forty pounds when I left. It's probably a hundred and thirty-five now."

Several hikers standing around cursed softly in disbelief.

"I haven't eaten hardly anything in the past five days," Coup said.

"No wonder it took you five days to get here," I said.

"Yeah. It was a little harder than I thought. I sort of miscalculated the weight versus miles thing, and I'm not moving nearly as fast as I had originally thought."

"If you're hungry, Pirate's got some spaghetti downstairs in the hostel."

"Starved. Let me make one more phone call, and I'll head down." Returning to his Blackberry, he made a hunchbacked waddle around the parking lot, still laughing at himself. "Yeah, I made it. Yeah. Supposed to have happened sooner, I know. Almost killed me."

Coup's demeanor was warmer and less uptight than I remembered. I wondered whether it was his business success or the punishment of his recent hike that had mellowed him out. His business had done very well. Coup is the founder and president of GoLite, the most successful commercial producer of ultralight backpacking equipment in the United States.

About that time, Baltimore Jack came walking up through the breezeway and eyed Coup's pack lying victorious on the gravel pathway. He tried to pick it up.

"Holy crap. What is this guy thinking?" Baltimore asked, looking my way.

"That's what I said. You'll have to ask him."

Jack Tarlin, Baltimore Jack, has been hiking this Trail for the past twenty years. His famous trail name notwithstanding, he grew up in Cambridge, Massachusetts. His father was a graduate of Harvard and a professor of romance languages there, and his mother was a librarian. Jack himself holds a master's degree in medieval history, and he's a wandering encyclopedia of kings, queens, wars, and plagues; his head seems constantly to be buried in a book. What he calls his "last real job" was selling movies to chain video stores across the country. When the company wouldn't give him a leave of absence to hike the Appalachian Trail, he quit and absented himself permanently. Since then he has completed A.T. thru-hikes over and over again. He was married once and has one grown daughter; he speaks about her fondly and often.

In his younger days, the only time you would have seen Jack on the Trail was when he was passing you, puffing cigarette smoke like a freight train. He gave up the habit some time ago, but he drinks Jim Beam as well as ever, and he still keeps a pack of Camel Lights in his pack for hikers in need. Along with the smokes, he carries Appalachian Trail patches that he gives away as souvenirs to curious tourists and their kids. Over the years he has become the unofficial beat reporter for what is happening on the Trail. Demetri Coupounas was news, and Jack wanted the scoop.

Downstairs in the hostel, a group of hikers was finishing up dinner. Coup, having already heaped his plate with the last pound of spaghetti, was scraping the bottom of the pan for a few more ounces of sauce. Jack took a chair near Coup. He had his reporter face on and his baseball cap turned backward on his head. He had lined up some tough questions for the company honcho in the plastic rain suit.

"Coup, you can't be serious. A hundred-and-forty-pound pack. Six hundred twenty miles in forty days, no resupply. What the hell were you thinking?"

"Don't know," Coup burbled through a mouthful of spaghetti.

"Are you crazy or just stupid?"

Coup chowed down happily while a bunch of us took turns lobbing good-natured bombs at him.

"The head of GoLite packing a hundred and forty pounds. That's sort of like Ben & Jerry's sponsoring a Weight Watchers convention."

"It's like Rosie O'Donnell pitching Viagra."

"It's like Toby Keith covering Tupac."

"So, is there an ultraheavy backpacking movement now, too?"

"For winter hiking, do you recommend the anvil or the sixteen-ton safe?"

Coup's laughter was contagious, and he passed much of the evening making fun of himself, which endeared him to one and all. He hit it off especially with Baltimore Jack. It turned out they had grown up around some of the same parts of Massachusetts and had frequented a few of the same bars, so it wasn't long before they discovered they shared similar political views. They ranted and slapped each other on the back, moaning about their common enemies in Washington. Before long, nobody knew what the conversation was really about anymore.

After Coup cleaned his plate of spaghetti, he and Jack moved their interview to the store, where a small crowd watched, with some interest, as I packed up Coup's gear. He had decided to ship it back to Colorado instead of carrying it on the plane. I spent half an hour loading, taping, and weighing the three boxes needed, each box the size of a truck tire.

"Coup," I said, "you have indeed shattered a record today."

Coup asked how much it was. There was a murmur among the oddsmakers.

"One hundred thirty-six pounds"—there were hoots of amazement—"beating the old record by forty-seven pounds. You and GoLite now hold the record for the heaviest pack and for the most weight we ever shipped back home for anybody."

"That's a proud moment," he said, slapping his knee.

"You're officially an old-fashioned hiker, Coup," I said. "I think someday we might even carry GoLite in the store now."

Coup caught his ride back to Atlanta around ten o'clock that night, and I thought I had seen the last of him for a while, until the morning, when the phone rang almost exactly twelve hours after his departure. He was calling back to see if we had shipped his gear.

"Yeah, UPS picked it up about fifteen minutes ago. I can probably call my driver's cell phone and get him to bring it back. What's up?"

"I wanted to go hiking again, but not with all that gear. Going light this time."

"What you're saying is that your staff doesn't want you come back yet, right?"

Coup chuckled. "I just want to hike. Can you get it back?"

"Sure. Where are you at now?'

"Standing in the Atlanta airport."

"Okay, hop on the MARTA and head for the Lindbergh station. My dad is driving up this way in about an hour, and I'll have him pick you up there."

Coup arrived back at the shop a few hours later, and UPS returned his gear that afternoon. I loaned Coup my old truck, and over the next three days he stayed at the cabin just hanging out and arranging his gear for his shorter hike. On the fourth day, he almost left on that journey, although it was pouring rain. Still, he was standing in the breezeway, fully loaded and ready to go. Pirate was in the breezeway with him, leaning against the wall and puffing on his pipe. Coup was weighing his options, and finally consulted Pirate.

"Pirate, would you hike on a day like today?"

Pirate looked out one side of the breezeway, turned and looked out the other side, and said, "Nope. This would be a zero day."

"Yeah?"

And Pirate told him: "I think you could use a couple more zero days."

Coup spent another two nights at the cabin and finally went through the breezeway smiling, just light enough in both weight and spirit.

Along with the familiar faces that would come and go and always return to Mountain Crossings, our complicated family managed to stay together that year.

Alpine and Jennifer did reach an agreement that they would not abandon each other. Alpine worked to patch the potholes in the far-flung road his life had traveled. He arranged to get the warrant for his arrest lifted after he cleared a few of his bank accounts, and he was able to work out a payment plan with the state of Pennsylvania. The divorce with Mariek was nearly complete, minus a few signatures on some paperwork. The meddling of Max, the pissed-off father-in-law, however devilish in its intent, was angelic in its effect; in an indirect way, Max helped give Alpine his life back.

The daughter in Norway remained a point of contention between Jennifer and Alpine, a difference in parental instincts. Jennifer couldn't understand why a man would not want to see his own daughter; Alpine didn't wish to disrupt the life of a girl who had never known him and might not even be aware that he still existed. But where Sergeant Ingram used to shoot at his disagreements, and Jimmy used to run away from his, Alpine—the full-grown man, formed at last from the best of the soldier and the best of the boy—stayed with Jennifer, loved her, and found a love worth its disagreements.

As for Billy, it was a sunny morning when he left us this time, though we knew he would be back. The air was a little crisper than it had been the day before, and the trees wore their boldest fall oranges, reds, and yellows. Sky was already outside playing with our new puppy, Patches, when I stepped out of the house and into the breezeway. Billy's old red pack was leaning underneath the white blaze painted on the stone wall of the south entrance of the breezeway.

He was about to leave, and if I didn't track him down, he wouldn't say good-bye. He never did.

I found him down below the stairs outside the hostel. He and Pirate were sitting in two of the three rocking chairs; they'd left me the one in the middle. Sky ran down the stairs after me, leaving the puppy stranded at the top, and lay down at Billy's feet. We sat and drank coffee, admiring the trees. Pirate and Billy combed crumbs from their beards with their fingers.

I asked Billy which direction it would be: east, west, north, or south.

"North for a while. Then west, I suppose."

"How about you, Pirate?"

Pirate turned over the bowl of his pipe, then struck it with his lighter to knock out the ash. "Can't leave yet. Halloween's coming. It's my favorite holiday, you know."

I smiled. "The girls will be happy to hear that."

Billy said, "I left the flute in the shop, hanging on one of my old packs. You'll take care of it for me, won't you?"

"Of course. But I thought you were going to learn to play it."

"I'm going to learn everything I can," he said.

I told them I'd heard from Dartman, who had called to say that he and Ramblin Man would be back our way in a few months. Farsang would try to make it back as well. Squirrel was going to hike the PCT. They nodded—everybody knew this.

I asked Pirate if he knew when Wee Willie and Fat Chap were coming back.

"I reckon, whenever they get the urge to go bowling."

"Bowling?" asked Billy.

I explained: "Whenever Wee Willie or Fat Chap are coming to take Pirate off the mountain, they always tell him that they're going bowling. Sometimes Pirate could be bowling with those guys for months."

"Good bowlers take their time," Pirate said.

When the wind swung around and a single gust of warm air pushed past us from the south, following the Trail to Maine, we stood up together. Pirate and Billy shook hands, without any words of farewell. Their eyes sparkled briefly in communication, and then Pirate went in to cook breakfast.

Billy and I climbed the stairs to the breezeway, where he took up his pack. It gave me joy to see him adjusting the straps, getting his hat right, taking his grip on his staff, turning his feet to the Trail. He had a smile then that was just for himself—his private correspondence with the good world. I had almost forgotten how young and how delighted he seemed on his departure days. Under the weight of his pack, he was lighter; gazing far away up the path, he was home. When he was ready, he gave me a wink and a grin, and then he started off. He would not look back again.

Margie came out from the house and took my hand, and we watched Billy until he disappeared around the curve behind the old locust tree. I stood in the breezeway with my wife, and we inhaled the cool richness of autumn as we shared the Trail with Billy a moment longer—Earl Shaffer and Grandma Gatewood's Trail; Bill Irwin and Nimblewill Nomad's Trail; and yes, Lorac and Hobbs's Trail, Pirate's Trail, and Minnesota Smith's—and the Trail that belonged to my daughters and my beloved wife, who smiled sleepily and tugged my fingers to tell me it was time to go back inside.

Our Trail.

I left it by the door.

About the Author

Ever since starting his lawn-mowing business at age 10, Winton Porter has found it hard to stay indoors. At 21 he opened B. Bumblefoot and Co., producing hiking sticks for retailers throughout the southeastern United States. And for years he tried the corporate route—selling gear and managing operations at such retailers as REI in Chicago, Salt Lake City, and Atlanta. In 2001, at age 35, he ransacked his 401k and bought the venerable Mountain Crossings store, a hiker's mecca deep in the Georgia woods near the southern end of the Appalachian Trail. It's a blissful match for the lifelong outdoorsman and natural-born storyteller. Now called the Guru of the Appalachian Trail, Winton is famous for his "shakedowns" to help weary hikers lighten their loads. When he's not busy selling boots and shipping hikers' boxes home, he's writing about the zany adventurers that populate the trail and his store. Winton's memory for dialogue, eye for detail, compassion for those in trouble, and gift for humor come together in the 20 chapters that make up his first book, *Just Passin' Thru*.

The author takes a break by the "Iron Maiden" fireplace, a popular gathering spot at Mountain Crossings.

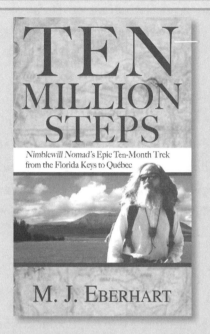

DEAR CUSTOMERS AND FRIENDS,

SUPPORTING YOUR INTEREST IN OUTDOOR ADVENTURE, travel, and an active lifestyle is central to our operations, from the authors we choose to the locations we detail to the way we design our books. Menasha Ridge Press was incorporated in 1982 by a group of veteran outdoorsmen and professional outfitters. For 25 years now, we've specialized in creating books that benefit the outdoors enthusiast.

Almost immediately, Menasha Ridge Press earned a reputation for revolutionizing outdoors- and travel-guidebook publishing. For such activities as canoeing, kayaking, hiking, backpacking, and mountain biking, we established new standards of quality that transformed the whole genre, resulting in outdoor-recreation guides of great sophistication and solid content. Menasha Ridge continues to be outdoor publishing's greatest innovator.

The folks at Menasha Ridge Press are as at home on a white-water river or mountain trail as they are editing a manuscript. The books we build for you are the best they can be, because we're responding to your needs. Plus, we use and depend on them ourselves.

We look forward to seeing you on the river or the trail. If you'd like to contact us directly, join in at www.trekalong.com or visit us at www.menasharidge.com. We thank you for your interest in our books and the natural world around us all.

SAFE TRAVELS,

**BOB SEHLINGER
PUBLISHER**